The Zodiac Experience

The Zodiac Experience

Initiation through the Twelve Signs

by
Patricia Crowther

SAMUEL WEISER, INC.

York Beach, Maine

First published in 1992 by
Samuel Weiser, Inc.
Box 612
York Beach, Maine 03910

Library of Congress Cataloging-In-Publication Data
Crowther, Patricia.
        The zodiac experience / Patricia Crowther.
        1. Zodiac. 2. Initiation rites. 3. Occultism. I. Title.
    BF1999.C748 1992
    133.5'2 – dc20   91-35179
                                                                CIP

ISBN 0-87728-739-2
BJ

Illustrations © Leon G. Dickens, 1992.

Cover painting is entitled "Sacred Clown,"
© Karen M. Sweikhardt, 1992.
Used by kind permission of the artist.

Printed in the United States of America

The paper used in this publication meets the minimum requirements
of the American National Standard for permanence of Paper for
Printed Library Materials Z39.48–1984.

As long as you are not aware of
the continual law of Die and Be Again,
you are merely a vague guest on a dark Earth.
                                    Goethe

Contents

Acknowledgments

I would like to extend grateful thanks to Leon G. Dickens for his tireless work interpreting my ideas for the illustrations in this book.

Thanks are also due to Leon G. Dickens, Jeanne D. Dickens and Peter Burford-Wood for contributing poetry appropriate to the zodiac.

I am also grateful to Peter Rendel for permission to quote from his book *Introduction to the Chakras* (London: Aquarian Press, 1974) and recently re-issued under the title *Understanding the Chakras*.

Thanks also to William Heinemann, Ltd, for permission to quote an extract from the poem "The Mystic's Prayer" by Fiona Macleod.

And to Elaine Prior for valuable criticism.

•   •   •

This book has been illustrated by Leon G. Dickens from original concepts by Patricia Crowther. "The Lady of the Night Sky" was conceived and designed by Leon G. Dickens.

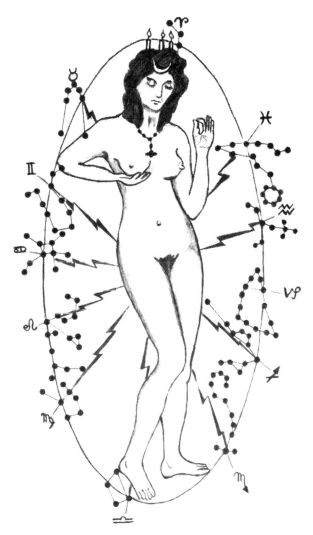

The goddess in her form of Lady of the Night Sky and
Mistress of the Inner Tides of Emotions and Destiny.
She spins her web from the center of the zodiac, with
the constellations shown as they would appear viewed
on the ecliptic—a strip of sky 18 degrees wide with the
Sun in the center.

INTRODUCTION

This is the beginning of a personal dedication of *self* towards spiritual development through the twelve signs of the zodiac; it is a form of self-initiation. It will benefit all students of esoterica who seek evolution in spiritual terms.

It is vital that readers be cognizant of their own astrological charts. It cannot be too strongly stressed that an accurate natal chart, calculated from the time and place of birth, can be an instructive manual for every avenue of life. A birth chart (or natal chart) can be obtained from a competent astrologer, without having to go into all the ramifications of learning the details of astrology so you can calculate your own. Among other things, the chart will reveal personality, potential, and the type of karma that has accumulated in previous lives on Earth, together with the reasons which have necessitated the present life.

Reincarnation is a common concept among those who study on the esoteric path. It implies that the soul experiences many lives, in many diverse conditions, and that for the soul to grow, it must be refined in the crucible of life. After all, *one* life, when viewed on a cosmic scale, can be likened to the flash of a meteor.

With each new incarnation, the soul faces a new set of circumstances, or circumstances similar to those of the previous life, if the lesson has not been learned. These can be interpreted from the natal chart, which forms a blueprint for this particular life.

The soul may "sleep" for many lives until realization dawns, when it "awakes" to take the helm of its ship and begins to steer its own course, with guidance from the Star Map. This may be likened to the manner in which a ship on the ocean takes directions from the stars, toward a safe harbor.

It must be understood, that the zodiac is a *symbolic* belt on the celestial sphere. It is centered on the ecliptic, which is the path of the Earth's orbit in space. Each sign in this belt contains thirty degrees and should not be confused with the moving constellations. You may ask, "How were the signs of the zodiac conceived?"

As far back as 8000 B.C., people looked to the heavens for guidance. Living beneath the open skies, we were—literally—at the mercy of the elements. Hence, phenomena such as thunder and lightning, rain and eclipses would rule and determine our fate. From early records, we know that the planets (including the Sun and Moon) were clearly identified as gods and goddesses. These beliefs arose because the planets seemed to have the power to change or intervene in human affairs.

In the Pelasgian creation myth, Eurynome, the Goddess of All Things, was the prime originator. She emerged from Chaos and created the Universe. The myth states that Eurynome also created the seven planetary powers and set a Titaness and a Titan over each of them.

The Chaldeans and Babylonians were among the forerunners of astrology and incorporated the twelve principal constellations when erecting their cosmological plan. These twelve constellations were the basis of the zodiac.

Star charts of the ancient Egyptians (from circa 4200 B.C.) have been passed down to us. But the earliest known pictorial representation of the zodiac was found on the ceiling of the Temple of Isis at Denderah, in

Egypt. It is now dated at 700 B.C., and is a most exquisite work of art.

The painted lid of a sarcophagus from the late Egyptian period displays the Goddess with the twelve signs plainly described around her figure. They are identical to the ancient Chaldean "road of life," but manifest a strong Greek influence.

The tomb of Rameses the Second (1300–1236 B.C.) in the Temple of Amon at Karnak, displays a relief that includes the four cardinal signs of the zodiac (Aries, Cancer, Libra and Capricornus). It has been assumed that this Pharoah brought these signs into being. This could be true because Rameses had a deep interest in astrology. He is shown in the relief holding the hand of the sky-goddess Hathor. However, we can safely propose that the zodiac did not come into being because certain constellations *looked* like symbols. They were designed to show the kind of cosmic energy operating at various times of the year.

The ram, for example, was chosen in order to depict the divine mind actually pushing life into manifestation. The driving force of the ram resides in its head and powerful horns. When it careens into an adversary, the head goes down and the resultant impact is colossal. The Sun, exalted in Aries, represents the Solar Logos coming into its own at the vernal equinox.

The bull was chosen for the second period of the year, when the initial impetus manifests on the material plane. It would be difficult to find an animal more representative of strength and fertility than the bull. It was an excellent choice for the time when the strong shoots begin to show in the dark earth and all nature heeds the call of the Sun.

The sign of Gemini, the twins, brings man and woman onto the stage to demonstrate their intellectual capacity as keepers of the Earth. Will they fulfill the trust placed in them? Will they protect their legacy? Although the twins have usually been shown as two males (*i.e.*, Caster and Pollux), most modern astrologers depict them as male and female. Certainly, the twins are the first human figures to appear in the zodiac. They are prospective mothers (Cancer) and fathers (Leo), not only of their own progeny, but of life itself! And so, the story unfolds and can be told on many different levels. You will encounter some of them in this book.

The influence of the Sun and Moon upon this spinning planet circling the Sun brings the changing seasons and affects our lives. The philosophical concept that each human being is a microcosm of the macrocosm—a minute replica of the universe—was part of the Hermetic texts, but this idea is a very ancient one. Before Christianity divorced us from our natural origins, the Old Religion maintained that people and nature were linked with the universe in a harmonious Dance of Life. Scholars through the ages have come to a similar conclusion.

> The celestial bodies are the cause of all that takes place in the sublunar world.
> —St. Thomas Aquinas (1225–1274)

> Those who deny the influence of the planets violate clear evidence which for educated people of sane judgment it is not suitable to contradict.
> —Tycho Brahe (1546–1601)

> A physician without a knowledge of astrology has no right to call himself a physician.
> —Hippocrates (born c. 460 B.C.)

Astrology produces joy by anticipation at the same time that it fortifies people against evil.
— Lucian of Samosata (A.D. 121–181)

Nothing exists nor happens in the visible sky that is not sensed in some hidden moment by the faculties of Earth and Nature.
— Johannes Kepler (1571–1630)

The universe may be not only queerer than we suppose, but queerer than we *can* suppose.
— J. S. Haldane (1860–1936)

The controls of life are structured as forms and nuclear arrangements, in a relation with the motions of the universe.
— Louis Pasteur (1822–1895)

In his startling book, *Introduction to the Chakras*, Peter Rendel discussess the flow of tattwic tides within the human body and says that they correspond to tides in the universe. These latter tides manifest as the planetary influences, the signs of the zodiac, and the seasons. Moreover, Mr. Rendel asserts that at the moment of birth, "we enter the flow of becoming." He also states that, "from a knowledge of astrology it is possible to predict the future events in any incarnation; even further, the time of future incarnations and under what signs they can be predicted." But the most amazing statement in the book is the following: "The universal Zodiac revolves in 25,550 years, giving each sign or age a span of approximately 2,145 years. This fact is, at present, much before the public eye as we leave the Piscean Age and approach the new Aquarian Age. The normal human breath rate of about 18 per minute also gives 25,550 breaths in a full day. Furthermore, 25,550 days gives a life span of 70 years (the average three score and ten for the Piscean age). Thus the rate of breath, length of life span and duration of universal Zodiac are all related in one rhythm."[1]

With this valuable information at hand, we can now move forward with confidence into *The Zodiac Experience*!

Initiation

The methods set out in this book are no different from other established ways of magical procedure. Where they depart from the norm is through the emphasis on the zodiac and its hitherto sadly neglected hidden teachings. By experiencing the Rites of the Zodiac, you will draw closer to the source of life itself, and align your own nature with that of the unmanifest world — the unseen energies of the cosmos.

The reasons behind all ritual is to extend the soul towards Godhead, by whatever name it is known. Thus, a positive attempt is given here to grow in every way and become greater human beings than we are at this moment. And that is no mean achievement.

The yearning for the spiritual is an inherent attribute in all of us and is the basis of all religion. But formal religion usually stifles this yearning by the imposition of dogma and theology. This is one of the reasons why so many young people are turning to meditation and astrology, because their minds are tuning in to new age thought. The Age of Aquarius stands for extension and an individualistic approach to the esoteric.

---

[1]Peter Rendel, *Introduction to the Chakras* (London: Aquarian Press, 1974); recently reissued under the title *Understanding the Chakras* as part of the Paths to the Inner Power Series (London: Aquarian Press, 1990), pp. 32, 92.

This yearning from within manifests as the phenomenon known to esoteric students as divine discontent. It is a very real condition and is recognized as the soul seeking attention—seeking sustenance. *The Zodiac Experience* is a firm stepping-stone in this direction, and can be used as a vehicle for the expansion of consciousness. What is astounding is the fact that the zodiac, evolved from the distant past, contains the qualities and potential inherent in the Aquarian Age for the next two thousand years!

An important part of any initiation is the focus on the *unusual*, where the mind is taken away from the mundane activities of life in order to prepare it for wider, more esoteric experiences. The mind must be shifted onto a new track more in keeping with individuality. An American friend of mine calls it "getting into second gear." Brains *can* become lazy, preferring not to work beyond the familiar, everyday scenes.

As an example, let's take the Initiation in Aries. Rising an hour or so before dawn and going to the special place that you have previously selected, carrying your items for the rite, may seem slightly perverse, but not impossibly difficult. When one contemplates the terrors of ancient initiations, it is relatively easy! But, if for any reason it is unrealistic for you to perform the initial six rituals outdoors, you will have to compromise. Deposit the tokens in a pot of earth, and in the Rite of Taurus, make the glyph of Taurus with sand or salt.

Among other things, people today are mollycoddled with wall-to-wall carpeting, central heating and a box which emits brightly colored pictures designed to keep the mind comforted—and for the same reasons that a baby is given a rattle! On the whole, this is done to keep people quiet and to stop them interfering in matters that do not concern them. It is no wonder that some teachers have decided to water-down initiations so that newcomers will not be unnecessarily alarmed at "unseemly" goings on!

As a result, most initiations have lost the vital ingredients of joy and terror, which made them *initiations*. What is left? A pleasant, coy, convivial occasion that assures the neophyte that they are with folk who are solely concerned with their nice, respectable group and who have as much idea of what an initiation involves as the average man-in-the-street! Fortunately, there are pockets of resistance, and souls who demand a lot more! I hope that *you* are such a soul!

After the initiation in Aries, you will discover that the rituals and visualizations in each of the following signs become progressively longer. Aries is the sign of initiation—the starting point in the nature year and something to meditate upon. It is for students who are just entering their magical careers, and it provides the time necessary to absorb the meaning of the rituals and to become familiar with magical working and procedure.

The first six astrological signs express the physical world and our place within the scheme of things. As you are a child of the earth, it is right that the rituals be performed outdoors, close to nature. It is also necessary for the tokens and libations to go directly *into* the earth at the moment of initiation. In most of the outdoor visualizations, you will find that the gods and goddesses come to you, but in the six spiritual signs from Libra onwards, you journey to meet the gods and goddesses and return the same way. These latter visualizations are more involved, but take place in the comfort of your home. The power and beneficence of these images cannot be too strongly stressed. Whether they be recognized as gods and goddesses, or intelligences of pure force, is immaterial. They have nursed humanity forward from the beginning of time and an acknowledgment of their existence will forge a personal link of inestimable value for the future.

Do not worry if you are new to this type of concentration, or "seeing" in the mind. Before attempting a visualization you can read it through many times in order to become *en rapport* with the scenes and images. This will also help develop and train the mind. Magical work, like any other skill, needs practice and more practice, in order to achieve proficiency.

When actually performing a visualization, the scenes may be viewed on a mental screen as if observing a film, although you will find that they are constructed so as to make *you* the chief participant! It is important to understand that all mental image-making is closely linked to the astral levels. All thought-forms impinge upon the astral, which links with the Inner Dimensions of the element water and is, therefore, fluidic and plastic. The astral body is of a similar substance to that of the astral plane. It extends from ten to twelve inches around the physical vehicle and changes color according to the emotions and feelings of the individual. It is also known as the auric sheath.

It can be difficult for some people to hold a mental image for any length of time. As soon as the concentration falters, the pictures fade, and/or are replaced by an incongruous image from the mundane world. If this occurs, bring your determination and strength of will to bear. Clear the mind and build the scene again, from the place where it disintegrated, or better still, re-build it from the beginning.

A heavy meal immediately prior to a working is definitely not recommended, and neither is the partaking of alcohol. It must also be observed that the subjective world is to be kept strictly in its place and not allowed to intrude onto the mundane levels of life. These are basic rules understood by the majority of occultists, but are included here for the benefit of newcomers to magical work. All experiences should be recorded in a private diary, reserved solely for *The Zodiac Experience*.

An important part of this book is concerned with zodiacal traits. Although most people display *some* negative traits, you will find that, as you progress, glaring weaknesses gradually disappear. And, what is more, you will be consciously aware of this happening! For instance, when a situation, to which you reacted badly in the past, occurs again, you will find that your reactions to it are totally changed—for the better! Mentally, a breaking system will spring into action and the engine of thought that governs your emotions will suddenly be shunted onto another track and away from danger! All this will happen in an instant and your response to the situation will startle you because of its sanity, tactfulness and control. You will literally stand aside from yourself, so to speak, and watch this happening!

When a positive zodiacal trait has been chosen, and time is spent on its development, it will become rooted in the subconscious and flower in your personality. Care must be taken—even with positive traits—they must be controlled to blend with your other qualities.

For Aries, look through the list of positive traits and see if there are any you lack. If you are couched in these, well and good. Another sign may contain a trait which you need and so you will have to wait until the Sun passes through it on its apparent journey through space. Once begun, however, development of the trait can continue indefinitely.

You will, hopefully, be aware of any negative traits which may have unwittingly clung to your persona, like greedy leeches. The more you give in to them, the more they will flourish and grow as weeds in an untended garden.

When you have concluded *The Zodiac Experience*, the Sun will once more stand in Aries. If you *will* to renew your dedication in this sign, then by all means do so. At least three years should be given to these paths, and while everyone must initially perform them alone, subsequent journeys through the zodiac can be experienced with other like-minded souls. The path of any particular sign may be repeated as often as willed, *providing the Sun is in that sign*. This is a personal matter, to be left entirely to the decision of the individual.

The benefits that can be obtained from these rites are many. They will allow the student to develop spiritually and will improve and enhance the character and the personality. The rites will also seed a sense of belonging to the universal scheme of things, and give a glimpse into the starry future already planned for the Children of Earth.

ARIES

MARCH 21ST– APRIL 20TH

Planet: Mars   Color: Scarlet
Jewel: Diamond   Metal: Iron
Number: 9   Flower: Gorse
Governs: Head   Herb: Rosemary

Positive Traits
Pioneering; adventurous; enterprising; courageous; highly energetic; freedom-loving; a go-getter; enthusiastic; full of sexual vitality.

Negative Traits
Selfish; impulsive; impatient; wanting everything—now; tactless; starts things, but does not finish them.

ARIES

Enter the Ram with a rush and a leap,
awakening the world from deepest sleep.
The gold of the Sun on horns and fleece,
disrupter, progenitor, disarmer of peace.
Marshall of movement—fiery charge,
vigor investing the will to enlarge.
Thought before action, word before deed,
energy sending, the life-giving seed.
Cardinal Fire, the heavenly gift;
Initiative urging us all to uplift!

PATRICIA C. CROWTHER

ARIES

Aries is the first fire sign and the first cardinal sign of the zodiac. Ruled by Mars, Aries is the leader of the twelve signs and is known as the Herald of Spring and the trailblazer. This sign is the first of the three spiritual dispensations or outpourings from the godhead, that of Creation.

Aries' most familiar symbol is the Ram's Head, but another less well-known emblem is the up-springing Fountain of Life, which represents the life force of the whole nature year.

In the human anatomy, Aries rules the head, depicting the divine mind behind all manifestation. The ram was chosen as an apt reminder of this, the animal's power and force, when roused, being delivered through the forehead and the powerful curving horns.

Aries is also the guide, the its function is to lead — to set the pace — through the mystical mansions of the zodiac. Like the restless Ulysses, who, viewing the purple mountains on the horizon, cries passionately: "How dull it is to pause, to make an end, To rust unburnished, not to shine in use!"

This sign symbolizes the pure white fire of the spirit, leaping forward in an ardent desire for expression: fire, in its most energetic phase. But, for it to be the fire of love — its purest form — the soul must learn the lessons that Aries has to teach. Courage is one of the chief attributes here and can be likened to the magical sword wielded by the hero in legend. Learning how to use it wisely is one of these lessons.

In the Arthurian legend, the hero's sword is shattered and he is miraculously provided with a new one.

One, moreover, with magical powers! Arthur receives Excalibur from the Lady of the Lake but this wondrous, invincible weapon is only loaned to him upon certain conditions. And, so it is with Aries. As long as the selfishness, which is inherent here, is allowed to dominate the personality, no amount of enthusiasm and daring will avail the soul. It is necessary to realize that discrimination and wisdom *must* precede action, and that the storming of any citadel, whether it be a person or an idea, will come to nought if the sword is tinged with the rust of selfish desire. Boldness and audacity can be useful attributes, but only in certain unusual situations.

Sometimes, this wild impetuosity comes up against the Law of the Universe—the Law of Karma—and no matter how much the soul struggles, it is eventually forced to stop in its tracks and to reflect upon its apparent failure.

Once this self-examination takes place, the recklessness becomes steadied and more thought and preparation is put into future actions and enterprises. Excalibur can truly be named the Sword of Light; borne by the clear, steady flame of the Aries soul. At once illuminating and illustrious, it banishes the shadows of fear and illusion and none can stand against it. In this way, the soul sacrifices self for the benefit of humanity and earns that most elusive of dispensations—grace. This sign is known as the "Knight in Shining Armor!" *Aries symbolizes creation and resurrection.*

Legends

Greek
Phryxus was the son of Nephele and Athamas, King of Thebes, but because of the intrigues of his stepmother,

Ino, he was condemned to be sacrificed to Zeus. However, his mother, Nephele, stepped in and rescued
Phryxus and his sister, Helle. Hermes gave them the
gift of a fabulous ram which was endowed with reason
and speech and had a wonderful fleece of gold. It could
also move through the air with ease, so Phryxus and
Helle took to the skies upon the back of the animal. But
Helle became giddy and fell into the sea, and Phryxus
buried her upon the shore and named that place Hellespont. He then continued his journey and arrived safely
in Colchis, the kingdom of Aeetes, where he offered the
ram to Zeus. Its fleece was nailed to an oak tree in the
Grove of Mars and subsequently became the object of
Jason's quest.

Pelias, King of Iolcus in Thessaly, had taken the
throne from his brother, Aeson, who happened to be
Jason's father. When Jason was grown into manhood,
he demanded a share of the kingdom. This was not at
all to Pelias' liking so he said he would comply with the
request if Jason brought him the Golden Fleece — an
almost impossible task!

Jason built a ship and set forth for Colchis, and after
many adventures finally obtained the Fleece. He was
aided in his quest by Medea, the sorceress, who gave
him a potion with which to lull to sleep the monstrous
dragon which guarded it.

• • •

That the Ram was regarded as sacred, is attested by
Virgil (Aeneid, Book 7). He refers to priestesses of the
Goddess who slept on fleeces in order to obtain conver-
sation with the gods.

• • •

On the island of Crete, Pythagoras took part in a
ceremony of purification. This involved sleeping by the

sea under the Sun, and lying in contemplation by a river under the Moon, while wrapped in the fleece of a black lamb. Then, between night and day he went down into the tomb of Zeus to be made "at one" with the god.

•   •   •

In both Greece and Italy, prosperity and well-being was attributed to a ram with either a golden or purple fleece.

•   •   •

At the time of the rising of the dog star—the season of the greatest heat—youths would ascend Mount Pelion covered in skins from recently dead rams.

Egyptian
There were numerous sacred rams worshipped in ancient Egypt. They had many names according to locality, but they all appeared to stem from the earliest form of Horned God, known as Khnum. His real title was kept most secret and only revealed to the initiates of the mysteries.

Khnum belonged to the region of the First Cataract and was portrayed as a ram-headed deity with long, wavy horns. They very earliest Egyptians placed his chief sanctuary close to the source of their great river. The word *Khnum* means *the Moulder*, who had fashioned the cosmic egg on his potter's wheel. He was known as the "Potter who shaped men and modeled the gods," and he is said to have molded the limbs of Osiris.

He, it was, who shaped all flesh—the procreator who engendered gods and men. A most beautiful picture of him, attended by Isis and Nepthys, is painted on the wall of the tomb of Nefartary.

Another name of the god was Amoun who was worshipped at Karnak, and rams were religiously tended there as living incarnations of the god. The famous avenue of ram-headed sphinxes, leading to the great temple of Amoun, can be seen at Karnak, near Thebes.

The god's soul was considered to be present in a ram-headed sphinx—the combination of attributes portrayed by this symbol—containing all power, wisdom and mystery. In effect, Amoun *was* the life force. This is the god who was known as the "one who cometh at the voice of the poor."

Harsaphes, "He who is on his lake," was another ram-headed deity. His principal sanctuary was at Heracleopolis Magna in the Fayyum district of Egypt. From the earliest times he was given great veneration. King Ousaphais of the First Dynasty, consecrated a naos (inner sanctuary of the temple) to him.

Ba Neb Djedet was also a sacred ram. In common speech the name was contracted into Banaded, while in Greek it was rendered as Mendes. Herodotus wrongly calls this ram "the He-goat of Mendes," but inadvertently confirms the reverence in which it was held.

Celtic
The ram-headed serpent was an important symbol to the Celts. It appears as early as 700–650 B.C., and has been found in the grave goods of important personages of that time. That the Celts considered it to be divine is unquestionable because it was a companion of the gods and was prevalent in all their art-forms.

A particularly interesting statue of Cernunnos, "The Horned One," was found near Autun (Saone-at-Loire). He is seated in the customary cross-legged position and wears a long sleeveless robe, a torque (neck-ring), and a bracelet on his right arm. He is tricephalic and upon his forehead there are two holes for the insertion of horns. Cernunnos is feeding two ram-headed serpents which are entwined around his body.

The most famous representation of the ram-headed serpent is portrayed upon the Gundestrup cauldron where Cernunnos appears as "lord of the animals" and is holding this creature.

Italian

A very ancient rock carving from Val Camonica in northern Italy shows a version of the Horned God. Again, he is dressed in the long sleeveless robe with a torque on his right arm. He is accompanied by an indistinct creature, hanging by his side, which could well be the familiar horned serpent.

Tibetan

The Tibetans, who were rather timid of earth demons, would erect a ram's skull over the doors of their houses. These were ornamented with precious things made of turquoise and silver and were believed to have the power to avert any form of evil. The goddess Khon-Ma was regarded as the highest of the deities. Dressed in golden, glittering robes and holding a gilded noose, she rode on a proud ram.

The Rite of Aries

The Rite of Aries is the initiatory phase of the zodiac experience. Find a suitable outdoor site. Natural surroundings are necessary for some of these rites and being sure that you will be free from interruption is a vital prerequisite. You should be adequately attired for this type of working and should carry a blanket, or something similar to lie upon for the visualizations. Proceed to the site, before dawn on the vernal equinox,

with the intention of making the declaration c
not worry if the sky is overcast; it is the *tim*
Rite which is important.

When ready, face the East and declaim:

> "I contemplate the rising of our planetary star
> with awe, and realize that this same star is
> echoed in my body at the sphere of the heart.
> Thus, I identify with the Universe and claim the
> inherent right to progress and evolve with it."

Begin to walk slowly and deliberately toward the
Sun, feeling the warmth of its first rays on your skin.
Breathe deeply and allow your thoughts to dwell upon
outer space. Ponder on the millions of stars and planets,
whirling through inter-planetary darkness, making that
same darkness *visible*!

Sit down and allow your hands to touch the dew-
wet grass of your wet-nurse—Mother Earth—then lay
supine and close your eyes. Mentally examine your
body, allowing your mind to touch every part of it.
Begin with your feet and finish at the top of your head.
Feel the blood pulsating and the life-force flowing
between your physical, etheric, and astral sheaths.
Become aware of being an individual—of being unique!

Now, visualize Aries the Ram charging across the
sky; his fleece, gleaming and golden in the clear, bright
light. Even *he* is reincarnated at every vernal equinox!

This is the beginning of a new magical tide in your
life, so imagine the "Fountain of Life," bubbling and
rising within your being. Rise with it, and stand with
arms upraised to the vault of Heaven. Say:

> "I [_____ name] affirm my birthright at this Ver-
> nal Equinox and declare that my solemn intent

is to take initiation through the Girdle of Venus, the Starry Circle of the Zodiac. SO MOTE IT BE!"

Here, a candle should be lit, or a flame obtained by some other means and the mind brought to contemplate the wonder of fire. Remember that if our ancestors had not discovered it, through friction, its use would have remained, even now, a secret of the gods.

Lie down again, close your eyes, and begin the visualization.

♈ ♈ ♈ ♈

The God, Mars, comes striding over the horizon—a huge figure, with golden armor reflecting the Sun's brilliance. His flaming cloak flies behind him like some gigantic tropical bird. Mars turns and looks down, his sword held high in a huge brawny arm, his burnished shield hanging casually from the other. He throws back his head and laughs, and the god's raw power hits you full in the face. Suddenly, he points his sword directly at you and speaks—his voice, booming and echoing across the sky, reverberating in your inner ear.

"Puny mortal! Think not you can aspire to *my* stature. I mesh with the Sun, and sometimes, when my lust is strong—with the lady, Venus. But since you are here, mark well these words. Distrust any who would seek to subdue your spirit. Know your head to be the seat of divine illumination. Come quickly to this realization then walk between the Horns of the Ram and through the celestial circle. I DARE YOU!"

A bright red ray issues from the sword's tip and speeds through space. When it reaches you, it disperses in a fiery starburst which envelopes your entire body. A feeling of elation and power floods your being, and as Mars strides away, his laughter resounding like distant thunder, you automatically raise an arm in farewell.

Stand facing the Sun and declaim:

"I AM! And as the Sun enters Aries, I too enter into the sign of faith and sacrifice, through the primal element of fire. At this moment in my life, I initiate a new beginning, with new awareness. I will utilize the energy expressed in Aries, to burn away the dross of the old self, and forge a link with divine love."

A small token made from iron must be buried in the earth and the action should be accompanied by a short affirmation and a prayer. Use whichever words you feel are appropriate at this time.

These things accomplished, concentrate upon what you WILL to bring to fruition, as long as you are very sure it is within your capabilities to achieve at this moment in time. Begin to tread a round dance, making the buried object the center of your circumambulations, and at a reasonable distance from it. Use your own words, chant or song—whatever you feel to be right for the occasion.

At the end, stand with raised arms, in the circle you have created; look to the East, and say:

"The Earth around the primal Sun,
My sacred journey now begun,
O' Lord of Life look down on me,
And bless my soul's felicity."

TAURUS

APRIL 21ST–MAY 21ST

Planet: Venus
Jewel: Emerald
Number: 6
Governs: Neck, Thyroid

Color: Blue
Metal: Copper
Flower: Hawthorne
Herb: Lovage

Positive Traits

Practical; reliable; patient; great endurance; sense of values; love of luxury and good food; persistent; strong-willed; affectionate.

Negative Traits

Possessive; lazy; self-indulgent; a potential bore; greedy; stubborn; resentful; obsessed with routine.

TAURUS

The Goddess arrives! The Earth is born!
The sunlight gleams on the Bull's gold horn.
All nature stirs as Taurus is seen,
bearing Venus, the Earth's bright Queen.
The fire of Mars is lulled to rest
as he lays his head on her soft breast.
Lady of Love all hail to thee,
for Cupid's swift dart and the quickening tree.
Venus in Taurus shows the way,
to live our lives from day to day.
In sons and daughters of this sign
patience and loyalty in them shine.
Wisdom too is here aligned,
in the Sacred Bull all are combined.
Venus manifest in fertile Earth,
all her glories brings to birth!

PATRICIA C. CROWTHER

TAURUS

Taurus is the first fixed sign and the first earth sign of the zodiac. Its symbol is the Bull, representing fertility and the manifestation of everything in the natural world.

Venus, the love goddess, rules this sign, showing us that love is the motivating force. The horns of the bull symbolize the feminine orb—the Moon, which is exalted in Taurus. Another emblem is the Cornucopia—the Horn of Plenty.

Although it is an earth sign, Taurus has many spiritual aspirations which were recognized by the Babylonians in the winged bulls that guarded their temples.

The sign governs the throat, where lies the thyroid gland, the organizer of the body. The vocal chords are also here, enabling the mind to manifest its thoughts—for it is in Taurus that sound is born.

Fine arts of every description owe their beauty to Taurus and its ruler, Venus. Music, which by its very nature can stir the soul, and indeed the astral body, is one of the most ethereal of the arts. The sign is a constant reminder of reconciliation between the physical and the spiritual realms, and for this reason, it is one of the most holy in the zodiac.

The inertia of fixed earth is very great and often produces laziness or apathy, or that most difficult of traits—obstinacy. In this respect it can be frustratingly inflexible and slow at times and if accused of this, or asked to "get its finger out," will merely reply with a bovine stare, strangely reminiscent of the animal of this sign!

Rest is surely the most welcome of rewards when work is done, and does not imply a static condition but rather the building of further resources for future functioning. We must also remember that Taurus is the sign of labor. It is known as the Sign of the Builder and many souls have an inborn craving to work in stone or clay and to build beautiful and functional edifices for the benefit of their fellow human beings, for theirs is the sign of the artisan.

Of course, it is well known that most souls born under this sign have the gift of green fingers and find great satisfaction in gardening and looking after Mother Nature's kitchen. The obvious love that they feel for all growing things is apparent to all who know them.

The young soul is born in Taurus to learn the lessons of spiritual growth, with carefulness and precision. They can often be most painstaking in everything they attempt, but this must also be true of their soul-life. Very carefully, they must learn to apply control over the lower self so that it does not become the master, and this can be a difficult thing to accomplish. Nevertheless, with due diligence, the Inner Temple will grow, sometimes unconsciously, because of the service and help they give to others in the everyday world. All these things are important, for Taurus is the sign which reveals the glory of the spiritual, shining through the things of Earth.

The innate power of Taurus is colossal—a mighty reservoir to be tapped at will—and one in which the divine energy that is Aries takes on physical shape to become the great evolutionary storehouse coalescing spirit with matter.

Shades of blue, green and pink are the colors of Taurus. The blue of the forget-me-not, the green of young plants, and the pink of the wild rose. The dove is another symbol of Venus and reveals the peace inherent here. This sign is called the sign of Aphrodite. *Taurus symbolizes stability and growth.*

Legends

Egyptian

A sacred bull named Apis was honored throughout Egypt and worshipped at Memphis. His body was black and always distinguished by unique markings. A white triangle had to be upon his forehead; the image of a scarab upon his tongue; the shape of a vulture upon his back; his tail had to contain double hairs, and a mark like a crescent moon had to be on his right side. If these attributes were present, then the bull was regarded as being a repository for the soul of Osiris.

During the festival of Apis, which lasted for seven days, it was thought to be a great honor if the animal entered a house. The priests would lead the garlanded beast, in solemn procession, to the Nile, where Apis blessed the water by wading in it. If his term of office had ended, he would be drowned in the river and his body embalmed. Great were the lamentations in Egypt when he died, until another bull was found with identical markings upon it.

Vast subterranean chambers have been discovered at Sakkara, where mummified bodies of the sacred animals were buried in huge monolithic sarcophagi built of sandstone or pink granite. Above was the great temple. Apis literally became an Osiris and was venerated as Usar-Hapi and Osiris Apis.

As an animal of prophesy, the bull was used to predict future events. After placing money and incense upon his altar, those wishing to know the future would place an ear at the god's mouth. They would then leave the temple, stopping their ears until they had traced one hundred steps. The first sounds heard after that were interpreted as the answer of the oracle.

Greek

The bull was of great antiquity in the island of Crete. It was considered to be a sacred beast and one in which the god could dwell. The god was worshipped, together with the Great Goddess, and both had celestial origins. The Aegean godhead was known as Asterius (the starry) and curiously, within the constellation of Taurus is the star Aldebaran, which shines like a ruby. It is a star of the first magnitude and one of the brightest in the heavens. However, Asterius is the masculine form of Asterie, the ancient goddess who was Queen of Heaven, creatrix of the universe and ruler of the planetary powers.

Europa, the daughter of Agenor, King of Phoenicia and Telephassa, was so beautiful that Zeus became enamored of her. He assumed the shape of a snow-white bull and mingled with the herds of Agenor at a time when Europa and her female attendants were gathering flowers in the meadows. The girl's attention was caught by the white, glistening coat and the gentle, yet majestic mien of the beast. She caressed the animal and wove a garland of flowers, which she placed around its neck. The bull knelt before the princess and she ventured to climb upon its mighty back. Zeus immediately took advantage of the situation and trotting toward the shore, he suddenly plunged into the waves.

Terrified, Europa screamed and clung to the animal for dear life, but he carried her safely to Gortyna in Crete, where the god assumed his original shape and declared his love for the princess.

Europa became the mother of Minos, Sarpedon, and Rhadamanthus by Zeus, but later, she married Asterius, King of Crete, who adopted her children and esteemed them as his own. Tennyson alludes to the capture of Europa thus:

Sweet Europa's mantle blew unclasped,
From off her shoulder backward borne;
From one hand droop'd a crocus; one hand
    grasp'd
The mild Bull's golden horn[2]

The continent of Europe was named from these adventures of Europa!

Minos, the son of Europa, became King of Crete in his turn, and as a son of Zeus he was revered, but also feared. He it was who founded the famous labyrinth, the lair of the fabulous Minotaur. Some say that the labyrinth was another name for the Palace of Knossos itself. It certainly could answer to such a description, being compounded of hundreds of passages and alleyways. There were also extensive maze-like tunnels and rooms beneath the city.

The labyrinth was built for Minos by one Daedalus, an Athenian who was a master craftsman renowned for his ingenuity and dexterity. Daedalus killed his nephew, a rival craftsman, and sought sanctuary with Minos in Crete.

The story of how Theseus slayed the Minotaur, a creature half-man, half-bull, which lived in the center of the labyrinth, is well-known. Ariadne, the daughter of King Minos, helped her lover, Theseus, in his quest. She was given instructions by Daedalus on how the

---

[2]*The Poems of Tennyson*, Vol. 1, "The Palace of Art" (Essex, England: Longman Group, 1987), p. 445.

center of the maze could be reached. Daedalus also gave her a ball of twine to give to Theseus. One end was tied to the entrance of the labyrinth, so that the hero could take the ball of twine in with him and be able to find his way out again.

The Minotaur was the result of a union between Pasiphae, wife of Minos, and a bull. Poseidon, the sea-god, angered by Minos, had inspired Pasiphae with a perverse passion for the animal, which the hapless queen was unable to resist.

One of the most wonderful and amazing frescoes in the palace of Knossos depicts young maidens and men performing the most extraordinary feats of bull leaping. A bull is shown in the act of charging, while a girl grasps the great, curving horns and hangs onto them. Another acrobat is performing a backward somersault on the beast's broad back, his dark ringlets flying in the wind. A third performer stands behind the bull with outstretched arms, waiting to catch and steady the acrobat when he lands in the arena.

The dancers are clad in scanty apron-like coverings, which fasten round the waist, and short, gaiter-type boots which end just beneath the calf of the leg. These are molded to their legs and were probably made from fine, soft leather. They wear headbands to keep their long curls in place and gold bangles on their arms, while their breasts are uncovered.

The acrobat on the bull's back is colored, the conventional way the Cretans identified the sexes in paintings. The other two are pale-skinned girls and very pretty. The mottled brown-and-white bull's strength and majesty are apparent in this painting. An excellent specimen!

The grace and daring with which these feats of bravery were executed speak of long and arduous practice and dedication. The artist of this fresco has made the whole art of bull leaping come to life. In other paintings, the Great Goddess is seen presiding over the games, so it would appear that they were performed in her honor.

There could be a connection here between the games and the annual tribute of seven virgins and seven young men, imposed on Athens by Minos for the murder of Androgeus. Theseus is said to have taken the place of one of the seven youths, in order to kill the Minotaur. So, these young people *could* have been trained to join the celebrated bull-dancers. The cream of Athens' youth was taken to Crete to become food for the Minotaur, and, as such a dangerous sport undoubtedly claimed some lives, regular replacements would be necessary. The deaths were regarded as sacrifices to the Goddess—and caused by a bull!

The word Crete is a form of Craeia, meaning strong, or ruling goddess. It is likely that the name Minos, or Moon-being was a royal title, each king marrying the current Moon priestess of Knossos in a ritual as old as Crete itself.

Phoenician

The cuneiform tablets of Ras Shamrah speak of a mystic tradition already ancient by the 14th century B.C., and one which continued well into the era of Christianity.

The most important god of the Phoenicians was El. He was also the oldest and most honored, and he governed the whole of Canaan. His greatness was likened to the power of the bull, indeed one of his names was Bull or Bull-El. He existed before other gods were created and a stone carving shows the god wearing a helmet that holds four rows of bulls' horns in relief—the chief sign of divinity. Other gods are depicted standing upon the backs of bulls, or having these animals near them.

Celtic

The bull was a symbol used by the Celts in most of their art forms. A particularly fine portrayal of a sacrificial bull is to be found on the famous Gundestrup cauldron. This sad aspect of animal sacrifice was also featured at the *Bron Trograin* or Lammas Festival of the Celts. And in the ceremonies at Tara, when a new king was anointed, cattle were killed on the occasion of Beltane the first of May.

The Rite of Taurus

When the Sun has entered the sign of Taurus, return to your special place, some time during the hours of daylight. Stand on the spot where your token in buried and recall the dedication you made at your Initiation in Aries.

Then, using a trowel, or similar implement, begin to dig out a circle, tracing the original one you made with your dance in the previous rite. As an alternative to digging (though not as effective), earth can be collected from elsewhere and sprinkled to describe a circle, provided you collect it when the Sun is in Taurus.

When the circle is complete, add two crescents at one point of its circumference to make the glyph of Taurus. ♉ The horns on the glyph are the exaltation of the Moon, which lies in Taurus, and this symbol was known in ancient times as the Gate of Horn. Placed before the Byre of the Goddess, and later, at Stonehenge and elsewhere, it indicated the entrance to a religious site, and was, therefore, a sacred concept.

Stand in the circle you have made, facing the horns. Raise your arms in the form of twin crescents, hands curving inwards, and say:

"I come to learn the lessons of Taurus—the lessons of patience and endurance that the White Bull displays. The attributes of strength and perseverance must also become part of my character, so that I may evolve and continue in my Quest. I come to learn the true meaning of Love and to grow in Soul until the light of Love shines from within. I call upon Venus—the Goddess of Love! May she deign to look upon me and grant me a spark of that Divine Light."

Lie down, close your eyes, and begin the visualization.

A white cloud appears on the horizon. As it approaches, you realize that it is not a cloud at all, but a flight of doves. They circle high above your head and three of them alight on nearby trees, uttering their soft calls. You hear the lowing of an animal, and coming towards you is the White Bull itself, wearing a yoke of red roses and bearing upon its back a lady of exquisite beauty. She wears a gown of deep cornflower-blue, held in place by a bronze girdle embroidered with many-colored jewels. They flash and wink in the bright sunlight and dazzle you with their brilliance. A garland of roses is entwined in her luxuriant, red-gold hair and she carries a copper lamp in her hand.

From the surrounding greenery, small birds and animals begin to appear—drawn to their mistress and glad that she has come among them. The animals run to meet this welcome visitor, while the birds skim and flutter above the snow-white beast and its rider.

The Bull halts before the Gate of Horn, the golden horns bent, submissively, and the lady slips from its back and approaches the circle. She stands inside the Gate, and, smiling, proffers the Lamp. Stepping forward, your hands tremble as you receive the flame. The aura of the lady is vibrant and tantalizing in its power and the air is filled with her perfume. It is as though all the flowers in the world were present, and there is also a musky, animal scent, disturbing and strangely exciting. Your breath quickens and a light moisture breaks upon the surface of your body. You are very much aware that your sexuality has become aroused, and you are also aware that it is being evoked by the presence of Venus, for the lady is none other than the Goddess of Love, herself!

The Lamp feels cold between your fingers, and you kneel, regarding the flame with reverence. It glows and changes color—pink—gold—blue, and a vivid emerald green. It speaks of many things and it feeds your soul.

Eventually, you realize that Venus is holding out a white hand, and you give the Lamp back to her and thank her. When she speaks, her voice is soft and melodious and utterly compelling.

"In your quest for light, forget not the body. It needs be a fitting temple for the soul. Through the will and the higher self you must mold it so that it glorifies and serves the spirit. Gain mastery over the lower self and allow Taurus—the sign of the builder—to show the way.

"The Lamp of Life is carried within every man and woman and burns brightly when we truly love. Awaken, then, to fullest life through the

art of love which is the most sacred of all rites.
Let the flame burn in your breast and light the
way for others to follow. Use the Lamp when
you desire to know the hearts of others, or the
truth of a matter.

"Love all growing things – the kingdom of vegetation and the flowers. These sense love
through the touch of a hand. Once you have
won the trust of animals and birds they will
return your love, and unlike some humans, will
remain faithful all their days.

"I am Gloria Mundi! My essence is symbolized
by the Rose. Sometimes I am called forth by
dark rites, in the name of lust, yet such rites
never touch the Heart of the Rose.

"An animal's desire is quick and clean. It moves
in the name of its maker and there is holiness in
it. The White Bull portrays this truth in its garland of red roses. Bring me to dwell in your
heart and my beauty will shine from your eyes
and your features will be transformed,
thereafter."

You feel the touch of her hand upon your head, then
she turns away and springs lightly upon the bull's broad
back. Slowly, they depart into the distance and slowly,
you relax your mind and open your eyes. When you are
quite ready, stand up and declaim:

"Standing in the sign of Taurus, I dedicate my
body in service to my soul. Giving thanks for
this wondrous structure, I swear to use it with
discrimination and care, so that it may serve me
well in the years to come."

Pour mead (honeyed wine) into a goblet then raise it high and say:

> "I bless this Wine of Earth! May it sanctify my body and cheer me on the way of Light. Thanks be for knowledge received."

Drink deeply and be at peace.

Before leaving the circle, offer a libation to the Earth by pouring the remainder of the wine upon the ground, following the pattern of the symbol. The goblet may be refilled, if necessary! Then depart in silence and *look not back!*

GEMINI

MAY 22ND–JUNE 20TH

Planet: Mercury
Jewel: Agate
Number: 5
Governs: Arms, Hands,
    Nervous & Respiratory systems

Color: Yellow
Metal: Platinum
Flower: Wild Rose
Herb: Lavender

Positive Traits
Adaptable; versatile; intellectual; witty; logical; lively; young at heart; spontaneous; flair for writing and/or language; up-to-date.

Negative Traits
Changeable; restless, cunning; inquisitive; inconsistent; superficial.

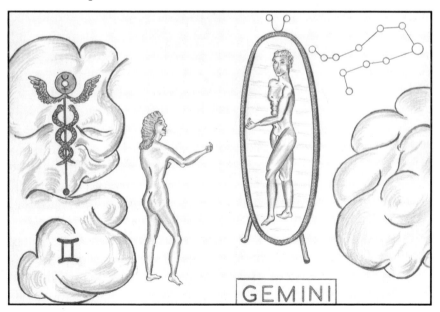

GEMINI

Blithe Twins of Air uphold thy sway,
cobwebs of ignorance sweeping away.
Androgynous once, in close embrace,
divinity, giving, the human race.
Alchemical change was in thy birth,
two of the earliest gods on earth.
Castor and Pollux, Michael and George,
spirit and matter released from the forge.
Hermes, thy ruler, Caduceus brings,
showing the nature of manifest things.
Lion and Unicorn, Sun and Moon,
unite in the Zodiac, May to June.

PATRICIA C. CROWTHER

GEMINI

Gemini is the first mutable and the first air sign of the zodiac. The Twins show the dual sides of the nature and also the higher and lower mind, which is separate, yet united, through the breath of life. The sign is ruled by Mercury, the winged messenger of the gods; the walker on the wind, with his caduceus of intellect and healing. Mercury is also the Psychopompus, the guide to souls on their journey from this world to the next.

The twin Serpents entwined on the caduceus symbolize the blending of the twin forces behind Nature—male and female, positive and negative, light and dark, Sun and Moon. Here, they find harmonious resolution in the golden-winged caduceus. Both the lion and the unicorn illustrate the merging of these cosmic principles. The lion stands for Love and power descending, while the unicorn represents the virginal, primordial state of original matter—the Prime Receiver.

Gemini has a special rapport with animals and seeks to form a bridge of communication and understanding with the animal kingdom.

Mercury's territory is the telephone, newspapers, radio and television, and as the first human sign of the zodiac, it governs the necessary equipment that allows the human being to reason, communicate and consciously memorize experiences. The "equipment" includes the brain, the nervous system and the power of speech. The hands are also an important feature of this sign, expressing the power of thought and learning through the written word. The hands transfer messages from the brain, conveying to the world the most exquisite music, poetry and painting. They can be truly described as one of the most miraculous parts of the human body.

In Gemini, the young soul craves variety and attention and is forever on the move, searching, always searching, for the new or unusual. Geminians love to talk and chatter on aimlessly to anyone who cares to listen. Literature holds them in thrall, and the mind, seizing upon the written word, is almost intoxicated with the joy of discovery.

Geminis must travel, moving from place to place, always delighting in new scenery and the new friend or acquaintance. The restless, changeable nature often brings criticism and the epithet of butterfly is bestowed, inferring a general fickleness of character. Be that as it may, this air sign must always move whither the wind blows. Like its ruler, with winged helmet and sandals, the soul must function on the mental level, darting here and there, seemingly in all directions at once, in order to stretch its wings and cover as much ground as possible.

There is a natural delight in words and the budding intellect has many choices at its disposal and many avenues to investigate along the road of discovery. Once the initial enthusiasm is exhausted, the soul is able to be more objective and selective in its choice of career. Even so, there will always be other diverse interests.

Gemini is the sign of the higher and lower mind and detractors will opine that there is a lack of feeling and emotional depth and hardly any staying power. But Gemini is always being pulled two ways at once and has to attempt to come to terms with the duality of its nature.

We must not forget that the social graces are born in this sign, together with the art of being able to mix at all levels of society. The distributive feelings of innocent love and friendship, like those felt in childhood, arise here. But, whatever comes, there is a quality of pureness in this soul which the world at large would do well to emulate.

The mature soul in Gemini will apply the mental prowess at its disposal towards pursuing the secrets of the universe, and will be drawn to science and other lofty, intellectual subjects. The mind, now honed and razor sharp, is able to communicate at levels unknown to other signs and can sometimes function as pure genius.

Impatient as ever, it abhors a slothful mentality and will cry passionately with the Persian poet, Omar Khayyam:

When all the Temple is prepared within
Why nods the drowsy Worshipper outside?

This sign is known as the child of the zodiac. *Gemini symbolizes differentiation*

Legends

Greek
Leda, a daughter of King Thestius, married Tyndarus, King of Sparta. She was seen bathing in the river Eruotas by Zeus, who fell in love with her. To obtain the object of his desire, he changed himself into a beautiful swan and, as a result of this union, Leda produced two eggs. From one on them sprang Pollux and Helena; from the other, Castor and Clytemnestra.

Mercury took the two boys, Castor and Pollux, to Pallene, a city near the Aegean sea, where they were educated. When the twins were grown, they accompanied Jason on his quest for the Golden Fleece and subsequently distinguished themselves in many battles, clearing the Hellespont and nearby seas of pirates.

During the Argonautic expedition, a violent storm arose, and at its height, two flames of fire appeared and played around the heads of the twins. In a moment, the storm died away and the seas became calm. As a result of this miracle, they became known as the Heavenly Twins and patrons of all seamen, their protection being invoked before every voyage.

As Horace wrote in the *Odes*:

So Leda's twins, bright shining, at their beck
Oft have delivered stricken barks from wreck.[3]

Macaulay refers to the power of the twins in his *Lays of Ancient Rome*:

Safe comes the ship to haven
Through billows and through gales,
If once the great Twin Brethren
Set shining on the sails.[4]

The twins were initiated into the mysteries of the Cabiri and were also admitted into the sacred rites at Eleusis. After death, they were deified, and Zeus placed them in the heavens under the name of Gemini. The Dioscuri, or Naked Horsemen, were reported to have appeared during battles, in order to lead certain armies

---

[3]Horace, *Odes*, quoted from Mary Proctor's *Evenings with the Stars* (London: Cassell & Co., 1924), p. 200. Readers may want to refer to the original in *Odes and Epodes*, English translation by C.E. Bennett and published by William Heinemann, London, and Cambridge, MA, 1964.

[4]Lord T.B. Macaulay, *Lays of Ancient Rome* (London: Cassell & Co., 1954), p. 80. This work is also published by Everyman's Library under the title of *Miscellaneous Essays: Lays of Ancient Rome & Miscellaneous Poems*.

to victory. Always, they were seen at the head of the troops, mounted on white horses, with spears in their hands and starry bonnets upon their heads.

There were many ancient shrines to the Heavenly Twins, but these were gradually Christianized. A notable one was the shrine of Castor and Pollux at Constantinople, on the Bosphorus, which became the church of the twin saints, Cosmos and Damien!

European
The Great Twin Brethren have been known throughout the world from around 2500 B.C. They were brought into Europe from Central Asia by a civilization as advanced as those of Sumeria and Egypt, and their names, at that time, were Mi-Ki-Gal and Gorgos. Mi-Ki-Gal became Michael, and in Britain, his chief festivals were Midsummer, when he slew the Dragon, and the Harvest, when he was the God of Fertility. Gorgos became George and he was allocated the humble role of leader of the workers. He was recognized as a jester or fool, thus, "Mad St. George."

The twins were transformed into saints under the Roman Church and their symbol, that of a red cross on a white background, was incorporated into the Union Jack. Their powers included healing the sick, protecting sailors, promoting fertility and appearing during battles as harbingers of victory.

The spiritual twin, Michael, became the patron saint of Britain and appeared on the coinage, naked, and fighting the dragon. In the process of time, however, there was a changeover which declared that George, the human twin, had supplanted his brother, and George did indeed become Britain's patron saint. Thus, the worldwide legend of the human twin supplanting the divine one has been enacted in Britain. Like Esau and Jacob; Bacchus and Pluto, the human has replaced the divine. The concept of material wealth has assumed more importance than the idea of a spiritual evolution in which the Light Bearer is predominant.

It is perhaps significant, that unlike the legend of Romulus and Remus, the legends concerning Michael and George have been allowed to fade from the memory and consciousness.

Italian

Romulus and Remus were the twin sons of Mars and Rhea. Mars was violently enamored of the Vestal Virgin, Rhea Silvia, daughter of Numitor, King of Alba. Unable to suppress his desire, Mars waited until Rhea was sleeping—then surprised her! When they were born, the twin boys were an embarrassment to the priestess. Therefore, like Moses, they were placed in a winnowing basket and pushed out to float on the river Tiber. But, due to sudden rainstorms, the Tiber overflowed and deposited the twins onto dry land at the foot of the Palatine Hill and close to a grotto named Lupercal. Hearing the babies' cries, a she-wolf investigated and found them. She dragged the basket into the shelter of a fig tree and began to suckle them. Eventually, they were found, none the worse for their adventures, by Faustulus, a local shepherd, who took the twins home to his wife, Acca Larentia.

From these humble beginnings, Romulus and Remus grew to manhood. When they discussed the idea of founding a new city, they began by studying the flight of birds. With the aid of the Augur's wand they divided the sky into two sections, then watched. In the part of the sky apportioned to Romulus, twelve vultures appeared, while in Remus' section, there were only six. Thereupon, Romulus harnessed a white cow and a white bull to a plough and proceeded to cut a furrow in order to mark the boundary of the future city's walls.

Not well pleased, Remus hopped over the furrow to show his contempt for the idea. This action enraged Romulus who forthwith attacked and killed his brother.

In 753 B.C., Romulus duly built his city near the Palatine Hill. Later, his father, Mars, was to have a temple raised to him on this very hill—in the days when he was a god of fertility, rather than of battles. Romulus needed to populate his new city, but the locals were wary of this man who lived like an outlaw, and they refused to cooperate. So, he took advantage of the festival of Consualia to abduct the maidens of the Sabine family who were his guests on this occasion. From there onwards the story becomes very hazy. Some say that Romulus was murdered by the irate fathers of the maidens concerned. Others say that he had to die young in order to be deified. But, all are agreed that he disappeared during a storm and that the city of Rome (after Romulus) is one of the greatest in the world.

The Rite of Gemini

When the Sun stands in the sign of Gemini, proceed to your special consecrated site. You can perform this rite in the daytime or at night, as you prefer, the sole proviso being the weather! Anything, from a strong breeze to a blustery wind should be blowing.

Stand in the circle and quiet your mind. Feel the wind upon your face and lifting your hair. Breathe deeply and become *en rapport* with this element.

When ready, light some incense (which can be in the form of a joss-stick). You are going to address the Four Winds, so present the incense to the East, and say:

"Wind from the East! you blow from the ancient lands which saw the birth of astrology and many other sciences. Let a breath of that wisdom imbue my spirit and aid my understanding of life. Wind from the East—pass on!"

Step to the South, and say:

"Wind from the South! Your zephyrs warm and cheer me and speak of indolence and ease. Teach me to appreciate life to the full, taking time for pleasure and enjoyment. Wind from the South—pass on!"

At the West, say:

"Wind from the West! I greet you and the rain you bring. You refresh and renew all the Earth. Your waters are present in the womb at the beginning of life, and, when the time comes, the Waters of Lethe take the soul to the Summerlands until the next incarnation. Wind from the West—pass on!"

Turn to the North and say:

"Wind from the North! Your coldness speaks of snow and icy wastes. Yet, from the North flow the magnetic forces—the powers of the Earth! Through ages gone, people have held you in awe and known your place to be the Home of the Gods and the Castle of the Stars. Wind from the North—pass on!"

Place the incense on the ground and stand in the center of the circle. Say:

"I call the Walker on the Wind! Hear me! I seek knowledge through the spoken and written word. Through discourse, men and women discover themselves. One mind exerts pressure upon another and brings forth new revelations. I honor and follow in the steps of my peers, while retaining my own identity. Therefore, O Messenger—heed me!"

Strangely, a feeling of desolation sweeps over you. What on earth are you doing, standing in the middle of nowhere, talking to yourself? This sudden change of attitude is the mundane in you, challenging the mystical, and is often the reason why so many would-be occultists fall by the wayside. The mundane self is quite happy to be fed, cosseted and entertained. *It does not wish to be disturbed!* And so it is, for incarnation upon incarnation, until the will is strong enough, the mind free enough, to break from the incessant demands of the body. Think on this!

Make yourself comfortable, close your eyes, and begin the visualization.

♊ ♊ ♊ ♊

You hear the sound of hoofbeats, and there, coming toward you are two milk-white horses, galloping side by side. Their riders are two naked men. They wear Phrygian-style caps, carry spears, and around each of their heads is a bright aureole of light. Needless to say, their bearing is regal.

The riders rein in their steeds outside the circle; the horses rear up, white manes blowing in the wind. You gaze at this awe-inspiring spectacle, unable to do anything except stare! Handsome beyond belief, their faces shine with power. These are the Dioscuri—the Twin Horsemen!

They speak to you, yet not in words. The mode of contact is telepathy; each thought transferred from mind to mind with the utmost clarity and sounding as a silver bell which reverberates softly on your inner ear.

"As the ancient Savior Gods, we have been many things to many people and we are here to welcome you on your path through the zodiac and to explain the basic meanings of our symbol."

Employing their spears, the Twins draw the sigil of Gemini in the air. The two upright lines linked by lines of energy at the top and bottom. The symbol glows and pulsates with a pale golden light, as the Horsemen stand within its great gate.

The Godhead made everything dual — everything that *is* has its other side; the animus and the anima, the male and the female. The entire universe is erected upon the fusion of opposites. From the largest planet, to the smallest cell, the same process is enacted, ad infinitum.

"Therefore, look inside yourself and perceive that other shadowy self. It is of the opposite sex to that of your flesh. Learn to know it and allow it to grow. Learn to love it and you will find yourself healed of many negative traits. You will also discover why you react to similar traits in others! The result will be breadth of vision, understanding, and the cleansing of your aura. Heed the words which were placed above the doors of all temples of the Mysteries: *'Know thyself and thou shalt know the Universe.'* "

The Dioscuri raise their spears in farewell, then turn and ride away, but the glowing testament of the symbol remains.

The sound of happy children's voices can be heard in the distance. They chatter and laugh as they draw nearer. Some play with balls, while others have skipping ropes and balloons. Their faces are radiant and full of innocent pleasure. When they see you, they come running through the Gemini symbol and crowd round, talking excitedly.

Although they come from many cultures, they understand each other perfectly. Taking your hands, they lead you into a dance; twisting and turning around the circle. Their youthful exuberance and zest for life is infectious, and you enter their mood with a will.

A boy with long golden curls and sea-green eyes approaches. His young tanned body is covered by a leopard skin. "My Guardian conveys messages between the worlds. I am the child—Dionysus. Forget earthly sorrows. Come, drink from the Cup." He offers you a golden goblet and you partake of the crimson-hued wine of ancient Hellas. Then, Dionysus calls to the children and small arms entwine around you as they take their leave. They promise to return when you call them. You are alone again, but the memory of those flower-like faces will not fade and you will never be lonely again.

A vivid flash, as bright as the Sun, is momentarily dazzling and you cover your eyes. There is a whirring, as of many wings above you and a laugh that is at once amused and mocking. You look up, in time to see something in a sun-bright orange cloak skim past. It flashes over you again, too fast to make out any form.

"Stop playing games and show yourself!" You gasp, horrified at your temerity. Did you really say that?

"No. You merely thought it," says a melodious voice just behind you. Spinning round, you behold the god, Mercury! The clear grey eyes sweep over you and seem to pierce your very soul. The god is clad in a short silver tunic and has winged sandals on his feet. He wears the winged helmet and carries the caduceus, his orange-colored cloak hanging gracefully from slim shoulders.

"Yes, I *am* as you expected me to be." He grins, showing even white teeth. A sudden warmth suffuses your being and you find yourself blushing! "You *are* reading my thoughts," you declare, angrily.

"It is in my nature to do so," Mercury shrugs his shoulders and begins to look slightly bored. Consistency of temperament is not one of this god's attributes.

"Anyway, what do you want of me?"

You swallow hard, then explain that you have taken the Path of Initiation through the twelve signs of the zodiac; that you wish this to be known on the Inner Planes and by the Lords of Karma, but, that most of all, you request help in your task and throughout the journey. You wait for the answer. The Messenger's hand gently touches your arm.

"Put aside your fears, you have shown that pride is not one of your faults. It can be the worst stumbling block in life. Everyone has the right to ask for help — and it will be given, but the initial request for it is a prerequisite."

His mood has changed again and he is full of concern for you. He sits down and continues:

"The sign of Gemini is one of insatiable curiosity and avidity to *know*. It engenders a deep faith in things of the spirit and speaks of the dual nature in the human condition, about which the twins have spoken. The brain is divided into two hemispheres. The left side stresses the mundane, practical and scientific, while the right side emphasizes the artistic, poetic and mystical. There is usually a tendency to employ one side more than the other, and this manifests as a preference to write with the left or the right hand. Leanings to the *left* side of the brain will promote use of the *right* hand and vice-versa.

"As soon as the preference is exhibited, it reveals, to the knowledgeable in these matters, whether the child will be predominantly a feeling or a thinking individual. Sometimes, the child is ambidextrous—it uses both hands equally well, and if this is so, it evolves into a more unique human being. But, as you may imagine, the mass of humanity is immersed in physical sensation and so there is no choice, as such. The natal chart is the sole determining factor.

"At one time, not so long ago, children were forbidden to write with the left hand, as this hand was thought to be associated with evil— hence the word, sinistra, or sinister. It arose from the idea that all witches were left-handed, and thus connected, wrongly of course, with bad or negative things. Actually, just because a thing is negative, does not mean it is evil. Darkness is considered to be negative, and light positive, yet one is merely the reflection of the other. And the reason why witches were left-handed had nothing whatever to do with writing. Rather, it represented the right hemisphere of the brain and the link between that side and the esoteric.

"It is in the brain that the pineal gland resides. Situated centrally, it is aligned between the eyes, in the middle of the forehead. It is known as the Third Eye, which is why the ancient Egyptians and other peoples represented this gland pictorially as an ordinary eye and placed it upon the brow.

"This so-called third eye is the source of clairvoyance or clear-seeing. When this occurs, the vision beams out from the center of the forehead. It does not stem from the physical eyes, but from this curious gland, which has the ability to "see" past, present, or future conditions. But, because the knowledge of its powers has been deliberately lost, its psychic function has ceased to operate. If an individual is aware of its worth as an important part of the human body, it can be nursed into activity through meditation and ritual."

Mercury touches your forehead with the caduceus and you become conscious of a tingling sensation in that part of your face. He grins, "Until next time!" Then he is gone, but you catch a glimpse of the bright cloak far above you.

Around the circle, a faint glow begins. As the light grows stronger it forms a rainbow curtain of indescribable beauty. Colors are much more vibrant and vivid on astral levels, and for while, you gaze in wonder at this glorious vision. Eventually, the colors coalesce into a single ring, but of a brightness that is difficult to look upon—even through astral vision. As it holds you within its circumference, a feeling of warmth and love, such as you have never known, pervades your being and tears of joy course down your cheeks.

At last the vision fades, and slowly, you become conscious of your ordinary surroundings. Partake of some refreshments and relax. If you wish to pursue some personal work, now is the time to do it. Before you leave the circle, acknowledge the Four Winds in the following manner:

"Winds of the East, South, West, and North,
a blessing on you going forth.
Through trees you sing, o'er hills you sigh,
and change the oceans moods and cry
in caverns dark, on mountains high,
you speed the clouds across the sky."

CANCER

JUNE 21ST–JULY 22ND

Planet: Moon
Jewel: Moonstone
Number: 2
Governs: Breasts, Stomach, Alimentary system

Color: Violet
Metal: Silver
Flower: Waterlily
Herb: Balm

Positive Traits
Kind; sensitive; sympathetic; protective; cautious; tenacious; shrewd; strong maternal or paternal instincts.

Negative Traits
Touchy; moody; unforgiving; self-pitying; untidy; smug; unfeeling.

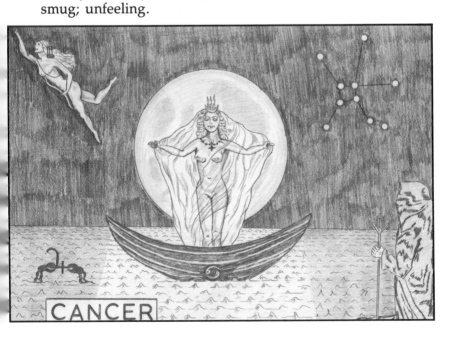

CANCER

O' Crab tenacious thou dost crawl
in oceans wide and deep,
drawn by the tides and the bright Moon's call,
while the world is lost in sleep.
Mother holding, arms enfolding
the bright-eyed babe new-borne,
may we uphold thy graciousness
when from thy body, torn.
Shielding, caring, ever bearing,
without a word or plea,
throughout the world's long history,
our praises go to thee.
Through thee souls catch the gift of life,
a never ending birth,
O' goddess Moon we pray to thee,
for mothers here on earth.
In ancient rites on lonely hills,
or in the forest, dark,
we praise the Magna Mater,
her tree, and sacred Barque.
Along the pathway, glittering,
upon the ocean's breast,
we hope for rest and rebirth
with the souls we love the best.

PATRICIA C. CROWTHER

CANCER

Cancer is the first water sign and second cardinal sign of the zodiac. Its ruler, the Moon, Mistress of Magic, is the feminine orb and controls the tides of the sea, the menstrual cycle, and the actions of crustaceans, birth, and all the fluids in the human, animal and plant kingdoms.

In the northern hemisphere the entry of the Sun into Cancer heralds the Summer Solstice, or the longest day. The Sun has reached the most northerly point of its journey and from now on, the days gradually become shorter. While the northern hemisphere bids him adieu, the southern hemisphere hails him as the newborn Sun.

The symbol of the Crab portrays the sensitive and vulnerable souls who build around themselves a shell of reserve and security. These natural home-lovers gather and collate information and knowledge, which is vigorously put forth when the time is right. Until that time, their home contains the necessary sustenance to outlast any invasion or threat.

Aside from the Crab, another, more esoteric symbol for this sign is the lotus, representing the soul. This beautiful plant grows in the mud (*earth*), rises through the *water* to the *air* and flowers in the *fire* of the Sun. Thus, the four basic elements are incorporated in this process.

The lotus, as an emblem of the soul, has been used in religious art over a vast period of time, most particularly in India, China and Egypt. Often, it signifies the yoni or female generative organ. The rose, too, is utilized for the same reasons. The male phallus or lingam is shown resting on, or in the center of, a crown of lotus petals.

In spite of being home-lovers, Cancerians are notorious for overseas travel. They must, of course, take as many of their family with them as are prepared to go, in order to assure themselves of a protective background.

In young souls, the feelings and emotions can be badly scarred by thoughtless friends and associates. If this happens, the soul will withdraw into itself, too frightened to emerge in case of further hurt. Very gradually, it learns to meet negativity and careless talk head-on, so that these slide harmlessly off the shell or outer mantle. One of the biggest faults in undeveloped souls is possessiveness. Once the crab pincer has grasped the desired object, it will not let go. It may be that in truth, it *cannot* let go, because it feels the object to be part of itself. Certainly, much anguish could be averted by self-study and awareness of this negative trait.

There is so much love locked up within the soul of Cancer that sometimes it just cannot bring forth the words to express what it feels. The emotions are strong—almost a physical blockage—where the soul can only stand, mute, the tears of tenderness and/or frustration being the sole outward sign of its terrible dilemma. And cardinal water *must* move—must deliver the goods!

This sign is intimately connected with the psychic and emotional vehicles of the human being. The soul is so sensitive it can pick up an atmosphere as easily as breathing. It is also extremely impressionable, as, like water, it absorbs like a sponge. It would be well for the young soul to stay inside the hard covering until it is absolutely sure of its surroundings and truly understands its position.

The immature soul must also beware of becoming smug. The adage, "a little learning is a dangerous thing" would be an apt synonym here. This kind of attitude can be caused by collecting and storing up against future famine and thinking that no one else knows what *it* knows.

A lesson to be learned here is the discovery of an inward serenity, a serenity that will manifest when the soul has become familiar with the heights and depths of emotional involvement. The mature soul will already have learned and absorbed the experiences and sensations of many lives and comes again to teach the wisdom of Cancer. At this point, the soul has poise and self-possession and the ability to send forth the light of the spirit. It can teach those in need what it has taken many lives to achieve.

Often, Cancerians gather about them students in search of knowledge. The radiance and peace shining from within is like a beacon to others, who sense intuitively that life-lessons can be learned from them. There are many advanced souls who are drawn to the medical profession and are doctors or nurses. The idea of a suffering humanity immediately calls forth those deep emotions of which this sign is capable. Maternal love and compassion flows out to heal and succour all. This sign is known as the "Gate of the Soul." *Cancer is the custodian of the zodiac.*

Legends

Of the Moon
The Moon Mother has been worshipped since the beginning of time by nations and peoples in every part of the world. She is the three-fold deity—maiden,

mother and crone—and the phases of the Moon epito-
mize her triune nature with constant regularity.

The Moon was recognized as the physical manifestation of the feminine principle, and of the godhead. As
virgin, she was remote; the untouchable goddess,
whose rites were performed by women at dead of night
and never witnessed by men.

Even as Mother, the goddess was still immaculate;
her divine child being born of herself at the Winter Solstice. This festival was observed in all parts of Europe
and in the Middle East. It was also celebrated at Alexan-
dria and there symbolized the rebirth of the Sun
through the grace of the goddess. It suggests the mystical birth of the fecundatory new light and the birth of
the luminous son, a matriarchal mystery which is
echoed in the words: "The virgin has given birth; the
light grows."

An Akkadian relief from the third millenium shows
the Mother Goddess presenting her divine son to the
worshippers. She is sitting on her altar and the Tree of
Life is behind her. There are many such representations
in different parts of the world. For example, a Minoan
seal-ring shows the adoration of the divine son. He
stands on his mother's knees, with arms raised, wel-
coming the stalwart, helmeted soldiers who have come
to worship him. A stone-ring from Naples, made nearly
two thousand years later, is uncannily similar to the
Minoan ring. The seal represents the adoration of the
three kings and shows Mary presenting Jesus to the
three visitors. The format of the two scenes is virtually
the same.

A most beautiful Hindu painting of the Goddess
and her son, depicts them sitting within a crescent
moon which culminates in an uroboric ring, symbolizing eternity. The signs of the zodiac are inscribed on the

circle and show the sovereignty of the Moon Goddess throughout the yearly cycle.

In many cultures, the crone aspect is still regarded as the terrible mother who waits in the darkness of the tomb; the terrifying One who ensnares her victims in a net. She is a monster and is portrayed as such in countries as far apart as Italy, Mexico, India and Egypt.

In Ireland, the crone becomes the banshee, a ghastly, dark, wailing apparition, warning of disaster and death. But in Western cultures, the dark mother is the repository of wisdom; the old woman, the weaver of spells and Queen of the Dead. She is also the Grand-Mother whose art is that of transformation.

The diversity in religious ideas and myths dictates the attributes of particular gods and goddesses. And yet, the Goddess, when stripped of all extraneous disguise, remains what she always was—the Goddess of the Moon and the Queen of Heaven.

Melanesian

In Malekula, the rites and beliefs have remained virtually unchanged since prehistoric times. There, the Terrible Goddess, in the form of a giant crab, still plays a big part in the lives of these people. She sits at the center of a labyrinth, and initiates into these mysteries must walk or dance their way through it. The mysteries, like those elsewhere, have to do with the progress of the soul through death to rebirth.

The labyrinth is situated near a cave and the presiding personage is always a woman. The goddess, or "crab woman" is named Le-hev-hev and she personifies the feminine negative powers. The Moon is intimately connected with Le-hev-hev and is shown as two crescents turned inward, portraying the lips of a great mouth—the dark gullet of death, which is the only way to rebirth. The twin crescents also symbolize the shear-like claws of the "crab woman."

This goddess appears on numerous clay jars and pots with the body or womb of a woman, whose home is in the depths of the sea. She devours in order to renew. Crab, tortoise and snail are often employed as symbols of the backward-moving lunar orb, as it returns to darkness.

Indian

In the ancient Tantric beliefs of the origins of mankind, the Great Goddess Tara is the source of all life. The White Tara represents the highest level of spiritual transformation the female can achieve.

Tara is worshipped as "she who in the mind of all Yogis leads out beyond the darkness of bondage, as the primordial force of self-mastery and redemption." She is the one who guides the soul over the river of death to the other side—which is nirvana. Her principal symbol is the lotus and souls nearing nirvana are likened to the lotus blossoms that emerge from the water and open their petals to the great light of heaven. Through life on Earth, the soul grows slowly. Fed and nurtured by the water of life, it puts forth a bud that will eventually become a blossom in the eternal light.

Tara holds the flowering lotus in her left hand—the lotus of a special psychic flowering, while her other hand is held in a gesture of invitation and giving. She encompasses the entire cosmic totality, from the mundane, right through to the highest spiritual attainment.

In this culture, the Tree of Life is expressed in a most exquisite form. The Earth is symbolized by a tortoise, supporting a lotus and a cobra (life and death). The crown of the tree is another lotus, where stands the sun lion (masculine spirit) and over this lion rises the Goddess, enthroned in light on her lotus chair. Tara-

Sophia carries flowers in her hands and around her is spread a golden canopy of light, in which gleam silvery star blossoms.

In the Hindu religion, the earliest portrayal of the lotus is found in a crown of flowers which adorns the head of a figure of the Great Earth Mother. The date of the statue is around 3000 B.C., and it was found at Mohenjo-Daro in the Indus Valley.

When Buddha was born, he immediately began to walk and at each step, a lotus sprang up as his feet touched the earth. Hence, it naturally became his symbol.

The familiar, "Om mani padme Hum" intoned while spinning the prayer wheel, means, "Jewel in the Lotus." Strictly speaking, "mani padme" is "jewel in the lotus," while the sound "Om" symbolizes the supreme origin—the Absolute. "Hum" is the embodiment of the spiritual within the physical—the eternal life force, manifesting in the ephemeral human being.

Egyptian
In ancient Egypt, the lotus symbolized creation and resurrection. And, because the white water lily grew on the reaches of the river Nile, it was prominent in all the ceremonies and paintings of these people. Over the centuries, it rose in popularity to become a common symbol for the afterlife.

The lotus was also used on social occasions and would adorn the dresses of both men and women. Single flowers might be presented to guests at a banquet, while an important personage would be given a necklace of blooms. When a single lotus was worn in the hair, or attached to a headdress, the flower would be placed so that it hung in the center of the forehead.

In one myth, a lotus opens to reveal a scarab which transforms itself into a divine child. The child weeps, and his tears become humanity. A variant of this is when the lotus rises out of the waters. The petals of the flower open to disclose a divine child, who is Ra, the Sun God.

The constellation of Cancer was sometimes represented by two turtles, called the Stars of the Water, or as Allul—a creature of the waters. But the most usual representation of Cancer was that of a scarab beetle. Indeed, it is shown thus in many of the Egyptian zodiacs. Its name, Kheprer(i) meant "to believe" or "to come into existence." The scarab lays its eggs in a ball of manure, created for this purpose. It digs a hole and proceeds to roll the ball into it, where the egg eventually develops into a newborn beetle. There are two distinct associations here: the scarab—a symbol of Cancer, and the ball of dung—a symbol of the Sun on its journey across the sky. Scarab amulets were placed over the heart of the dead as an emblem of rebirth and regeneration.

Greek
One of the labors of Hercules was to destroy a snake-like monster with many heads, called the Hydra, which lurked near lake Lerna in Peloponnesus. It seems that the Hydra's only friend was a humble crab, because, while Hercules was busy killing the monster, the goddess, Juno, jealous of his fame, sent an enormous sea-crab to bite his foot! Hercules soon dispatched this new enemy, and Juno, having failed to lessen the hero's esteem, placed the crab in the heavens among the other constellations.

Chaldean
To the Chaldeans, Cancer was said to be the "Gate of Men" through which souls descended from heaven into human bodies.

The Rite of Cancer

When the Sun has entered the sign of Cancer, proceed to your sacred site. Ideally, this rite should be performed exactly on the Summer Solstice. This is to be your first encounter with a cardinal water sign.

You must take with you a written declamation of your highest ideals and any aspirations begun at the Vernal Equinox. Place the papers in a small receptacle and put it somewhere in your clothing.

You need to bring a gift for the Moon Mother, the ruler of this sign. A bouquet made of nine different flowers and herbs is a suitable offering for her, as nine is the number of the Moon. You will need a small vase for the bouquet and should also bring some water from a running brook or river, and some salt with you.

When you reach your destination, place the vase of flowers in the center of the circle. They may be taken home at the end of the Rite and put in a special place. After all, it is the *intent* behind the action that is important.

Announce your presence in a way that you think fit, then stand with the flowers and say:

"I am here to learn the attributes of compassion and understanding which bind me to all souls borne of the Moon Mother. Gracious Goddess, show me the way to that abiding inner tranquillity which endures through any hardship of physical life."

With the special spring water, sprinkle the circle as follows:

"Be this circle blessed by the mysterious element of water, through which all life is born on

Earth. Holiest receiver of the precious seed, protect this sacred place."

Stand centrally, raise your arms and declaim:

"Great Mother of all! Comfort me in my quest and succour me through any trials. You, who are the essence of maternal love, and the source of all life, watch over me and guide me."

Now, inscribe the glyph of Cancer by pouring the salt upon the ground. The top line is made just north of the center of the circle; the bottom line, just south of the center, so that it encloses you and the flowers within it, thus: ♋

Read the written declamation aloud and meditate upon the task ahead. Then make yourself comfortable and begin the visualization.

♋ ♋ ♋ ♋

You open your inner eyes to find that you are in a lovely garden which is surrounded by a high stone wall. This is the Magic Garden in which the joys of Summer eternally abound. The atmosphere is one of great peace. A chorus of birdsong fills the air and small animals peep from the foliage, their bright eyes curious, yet unafraid. There are flowers of every description and color and their perfume is almost overpowering. Amid the verdant grass, a quiet pool reflects the brightness of the sun which shines directly overhead. Gleaming white waterlilies float on the smooth surface which is occasionally disturbed by a leaping frog, or toad. The garden gives forth an ambience of tranquillity which permeates to the very depths of your soul.

The emotions that arise have an appreciative quality, making you feel that you know this place in the here and now. The Magic Garden has become a part of your experience and you may capture it again, whenever you will.

As you walk around, touching the flowers and stroking the animals, you wonder if such a garden exists in the material world. It did, once, when time was young and the planet was unpolluted by selfish desires. But, as you can see, it has taken order and discipline to establish such a garden. It has been planned and brought into being by loving thoughts and careful work. In other words, it has been *constructed*, and has not come into being accidentally. And so it is with the Universe. It has been carefully planned and is in harmony with itself.

The garden draws you to it and you would be happy to stay there indefinitely, but you realize that it is growing dark and a little chill. The sun has gone down, the flowers have closed their petals, and the animals are asleep. Some glowworms attract your attention. They are busy signaling to each other near a bush which grows next to the wall. You walk over to them and discover a small door hidden behind the leaves.

Opening it, you find it leads to a wide expanse of seashore. The full moon has just risen and sits on the horizon, her light making a shining pathway on the dark surface of the sea. A huge crab scuttles sideways on the gleaming white sand, and you follow it to the water's edge. It disappears beneath the foam-flecked waves and, suddenly, you feel like dancing to express the feelings evoked by this enchanting scene.

Your bare feet weave a pattern on the sand and you sing softly to yourself. Then, a little out of breath, you sit down and gaze at the great orb of the moon.

There is something out there—a blob of blackness on the glittering sea-path. It comes nearer and you realize that it's a black boat with someone standing in the prow. Automatically, you stand up, too, and await its arrival on the shore.

Now you can see that the boat is shaped like a crescent moon. It stands a little way off the shore and the dark-robed figure beckons to you. The water swirls round your legs as you pull yourself over the side and sit down on the seat facing the figure at the prow.

The boat is apparently self-propelled as it moves off immediately, gliding smoothly over the sea. The figure is silent and does not move. Its head is covered by a dark veil and for some reason, you have a strong impression that you know this Being intimately. A feeling of coming home envelopes you and sudden, glad tears sting your eyes.

The light of the moon has dimmed. It now hangs above the ocean and has changed to a thin, waning crescent.

"I am the Great Mother, and this is my Moon Boat. I am come as Noah in my Arc of a thousand years, to succour you in your quest."

The voice is melodic, yet with a curious metallic ring to it, and it seems to issue from *inside* your head. A silver light emanates from the Goddess and envelopes Her in the shape of the *vesica pisces*—the feminine oval.

> "I have spoken to you in the aspect of physical love and now I am come as Mother. You are never alone! There is a unity in the universe and it is this Oneness of which you must become aware. The apparent diversity is but an expression of the ultimate—that which makes for life. You must look behind the mask of the manifest to find the reality—all else is impermanent.

"The divine spark dwells in all things, but in some species it sleeps, or is the overlord of a group, as in a hive of bees. The spark is shared between them and each bee is only whole when it is a part of the swarm. With animals, also, the herd share a group soul, but once an animal is separated, it lives to itself, and the spark within is fed by thought and reason, and initiates a separate existence of its own.

"In humans, each soul gathers experience as a bee gathers honey, though often not so sweet! In most humans, the spark sleeps through many lives until realization dawns. That awakening has come for you."

From the dark folds of her robe, the goddess holds out a gleaming, silver goblet, encrusted with precious stones. It is surrounded by an aura of violet light which pulsates and emits a sweet, low note.

"Drink of the Cup of Immortality — the Cup of Soma — brewed from the Moon Tree. The honey of the Moon brings you in touch with *that* which is termed soul. *That* which is free, indestructible and beyond all pairs of opposites."

You take — or do not take — the Cup. It is entirely a matter of choice. To drink is to receive that special initiation of the Goddess that bestows a wider, more impersonal vision of the feminine principle. It demands a certain subjugation of Self to that all-pervading power. It also gives the ability to transcend death and the ability to CREATE through the mens or mind — the fruitful inspiration!

At this time, you may speak to the Goddess of anything that is troubling you, or for which you cannot
discover a solution. The Goddess may even have a special message for you.

At last, the Goddess opens her arms and the dark
robe is caught by the wind and envelopes you within its
folds.

"Remember, you are never alone! I love you and I
am with you—always!" The words tremble on the edge
of your mind as you are carried away from the sea and
back to the now familiar Magic Garden.

The dawn chorus is in full song and the first rays of
the sun illuminate the tops of the trees. With a dor-
mouse curled up close by, you settle down in the grass
and close your eyes.

When you open them, you are once more within
your circle. Take time to accustom yourself to your surroundings, then stretch your limbs and partake of a
little nourishment in the form of bread and water.

Before leaving, give thanks for the Mother's help
and bury a small silver-colored coin (a silver sixpence or
a dime would be ideal), as a token of fealty.

LEO

JULY 23RD–AUGUST 22ND

Planet: Sun
Jewel: Peridot
Number: 1
Governs: Heart, Back

Color: Orange
Metal: Gold
Flower: Heliotrope
Herb: Borage

Positive Traits
Magnanimous; generous; creative; broadminded; good organizer; a natural leader.

Negative Traits
Dogmatic; pompous; snobbish; patronizing; conceited.

LEO

The golden, smiling sun on high,
Leo crowned at zenith rides
the tranquil path of Life's intent
and sits the rainbow's back with pride.
The Green Man's face in leafy frame,
as Summertime expands her lay,
appears to smile at Nature's game,
with flowers of gold and youth at play.
They risk the flame, as children do,
but fret not for the heat of sun:
Secure in faith and simple, true;
for God's their father and their son.
The pillar stands with real aplomb,
it's rampant strength endures all pain,
as we are born from Nature's womb,
to live, to die, and live again.

LEON G. AND JEANNE D. DICKENS

LEO

Leo is the second fire sign and the second fixed sign of the zodiac. Its ruler is the greater luminary, the Sun, which is the fixed center of light and life.

As the sign of Leo is the solar orb's own dominion, it is considered to be the royal sign of kingship. Certainly, it is the sign of the leader and links with the ancient concept known as the *sang real*, or the "Blood Royal." This concept has much to do with the legend of the four god-kings who came to Earth to mingle their blood with mortals. From this legend grew the idea of the Divine King who was put to death after a term of office in order to ensure prosperity for his people. As a willing sacrifice, his blood was spilled upon the earth to promote fertility and as a thanksgiving for the gift of life.

Leo is the second of the great spiritual dispensations—that of the Incarnation. As King of the Beasts, Leo equates with the solar deity, unfolding warmth and the flame of love—a flame which burns steadily at the center of our particular star system. At its best, this sign brings clarity and an inspiring radiance. Heroes of all descriptions are connected with Leo, as the positive traits are faith, love and courage.

The five senses are fully developed here, as is the sixth sense! Souls born under the influence of Leo have an inbuilt trust in life and the opportunity for being brilliantly creative. They exude confidence and affection and are frequently the "life" and "soul" of any group.

The power of the Sun-soul shines on all and draws many who benefit from such a benevolent heart. Children, particularly, sense the soul's honest simplicity and are happy to congregate round such an individual – the ever-young in heart.

These children of the Sun are born with a joyous sense of power and vitality, and as the Sun encompasses within itself all the colors of the spectrum, so this soul (according to its development), can have an instinctive noesis for harmonizing with each of the seven rays of progress.

For the advanced soul, the range of interests in life is titanic, as it switches easily, and often unconsciously, between teaching, art, philosophy, healing and mysticism. Everything that is interesting or thought-provoking comes within its provenance. The danger here, is that it may spread itself too thinly and cry, "Time! Oh, if only there was more time!"

As this sign governs the heart center, the soul intuitively senses that its true function is to sow the seeds of universal love. Leo also gives a sense of rightness and self-confidence and an innocence not quite of this world.

In terms of religious belief, it finds its own way, much to the perplexity of others. As a sign, it can be completely amoral, preferring to follow a personal code in life, which it discovers through an innate understanding of the Laws of the universe.

In the young soul, the air of self-assurance can manifest as false pride and a bombastic personality, because it senses, however dimly, the true glory of its birthright, yet cannot express itself in positive terms. The sense of power may become negated into showy ostentation or the soul may live in its own world of self-flattery and indulgence.

There is often a pretense of knowledge where none exists, and for a while, it may convince. But the flatterers and sycophants, drawn by the brightness and gaudy display—like moths attracted to a flame—will soon tire and desert this tiny light. And so it must be until the realization dawns that the first victory must be a victory over the kingdom of Self.

Then, too, the young soul, having an inborn sense of honor and a simple faith in itself and others, can easily be deceived. When the betrayal occurs, great is the indignation, giving way to sorrow and even rage. The whole gamut of emotions is played out to anyone with a sympathetic ear. (Leo is at its finest in the theater, with an audience!) And if a confrontation with the "guilty" party is inevitable, it will be the worse for this young soul, because in ordinary, everyday matters it finds it very difficult to win an argument. The young soul is so sure it is loved and idealized, it has no weapons of defense and will merely stand and roar quite impotently.

Slowly, the soul learns that its true vocation as a leader is to seek out the higher self—the Divine Fire—in others. By its own example of inspiration, tolerance and faith, the soul must put forth the flame of love and ignite that same flame within other hearts. With such altruistic aids at its disposal, it cannot fail to bring enlightenment to humanity.

The advanced soul in Leo strides confidently forward, with poised, erect mien, and that most important of attributes—*magnetism*.

This sign, more than the others, excels in invocation and prayer. Such a prayer might come from the pen of Fiona Macleod:

Lay me to sleep in sheltering flame
O Master of the Hidden Fire

Make pure my heart and cleanse for me
My soul's desire.[5]

This sign is called the Throne of the Sun. *Leo is the
dispensation of benevolence.*

Legends

Of the Goddess and the Lion

Throughout the Middle East, from time immemorial,
the Great Goddess has been associated with the King of
Beasts. Indeed, one of her many titles was the Lady of
the Beasts. In Crete, she plays with lions, or stands on a
mountain flanked by them. In Phrygia, these animals
accompany her, and on a bronze hydra from Greece,
she appears, winged, with four laughing lions standing
around her. From the same country, a bronze mirror
shows an elegant, slim goddess, standing on a crouch-
ing lion.

A later bronze, from the second century A.D.,
reveals Cybele, seated on a throne and being pulled
along on a four-wheeled cart by two lions. This theme is
shown in an Italian, medieval painting, where the goddess, Fortuna, is similarly enthroned. A peacock sits on
her right hand and in her left she carries a long, flowering scepter. A stone carving from Italy shows the goddess holding a lion in each hand. A 15th century tapes-
try depicts the Virgin Mary holding the infant Jesus.
She, too, is seated on a throne between two rampant
lions.

The famous Lion Gate at Mycenae still stands
before the ruins of the great palace. The lions stare

---

[5]Fiona Macleod, "The Mystic's Prayer," in *From the Hills of Dream*
(London: William Heinemann, 1907), p. 199.

towards the distant mountains and stand in an attentive position, their front paws resting on a single stone pillar.

Gate, pillar, tree and stone, were primordial symbols of the Goddess and, as such, were portrayed as representations of her. One of the earliest stone erections was of two pillars covered with a stone oblong and symbolizing her threefold aspect. The masculine principle was added later, as a lone, phallic upright stone. The Stone Gate could lead into byre, temple or sanctuary. It was the entrance to the Womb of the Goddess and therefore, the pillar between the sentinel lions at Mycenae expresses the numinous presence of the Goddess, herself.

In Babylon, Ishtar was Goddess of the Moon and Goddess of the Evening Star, and to the people, she was indeed a personification of the planet Venus, being a goddess of love. As a defender of her people, she goes forth as Lady of Battles. A stele from Tell Ahmar, eighth century B.C., shows her fully armed and standing upon her own sacred lion, the star of Venus shining on her brow. Sometimes Ishtar is seen driving a chariot, drawn by seven lions.

The Ishtar Gate of Babylon was a masterpiece of beauty and art. It was dedicated to the Goddess and spanned the processional way between the palace of Nebuchadnezzar and the temple of Marduk. The great double gates were decorated with paintings of animals in yellow, brown and white, upon a background of glazed blue bricks. It is dated between 604 and 561 B.C. Anyone visiting Germany can see a reconstruction of this marvelous gate at the Berlin Museum. The original glazed bricks have been incorporated in the reconstruction.

A huge stone lion was found in the ruins of the city of Babylon. It stands over the body of a man, with front feet placed one on either side of his head. Clearly, although in the act of dominating the man, the animal is not harming him. Archaeologists were unable to move the sculpture because it was so big. It still stands *in situ* among the ruins, tentatively dated around the first millennium B.C.

Greek

To kill and flay the Nemean lion was the first of the twelve tasks allotted to Hercules by Eurystheus, a king of Argos and Mycenae. The Pythoness at Delphi had advised Hercules to put himself at the king's disposal, to go to Tiryns forthwith, and perform twelve labors. The reward for such would be immortality.

The twelve labors could be likened to a form of initiation, and most probably were. Inasmuch as there were *twelve* tasks to perform, one could associate the labors of Hercules with the twelve signs of the zodiac. The feats involved were titanic and were performed entirely on the physical plane in the space of a few years!

The Nemean lion was huge and had a pelt which was invincible against bronze, iron and stone. Finding its lair after much difficulty, Hercules awaited the animal's arrival. The lion returned in the evening, its fur covered in blood from the day's killings. Hercules' arrows, however, glanced off the protective pelt, the beast not even appearing to notice them. It merely yawned and settled down, sleepy and replete.

Hercules attacked it with his sword, but the blade bent, and slid harmlessly aside. Aghast, the hero took up his club and dealt the lion a mighty blow on the muzzle, which made it shake its head and disappear into its lair—a double-mouthed cave.

The shattered club was abandoned as Hercules threw a net over one entrance of the cave, then entered by the other and began to wrestle with the animal. It bit off one of his fingers, but he held on, until he had strangled it.

Flaying the lion was another matter, but the problem was solved by employing the lion's own claws. Ever after, Hercules wore the invulnerable pelt in battle, and, it is said, he wore the head as a helmet.

Egyptian

Among their many deities, the Egyptians worshipped the lion-headed Sekhmet, a goddess of vengeance and punisher of the damned in the Underworld. But, above all, she was revered as the Goddess of Fire and symbolized the burning force of the Sun.

Originally, she was a divinity of Letopolis, then became Ptah's wife and bore him a son—Nefertum. With Ptah and Imhotep she was a member of the great Triad of Memphis.

Bast, although a member of the cat-family, was a gentler aspect of Sekhmet, personifying the life-giving warmth of the Sun. She was the protectress of the domestic cat and is shown holding her basket of kittens with either a sistrum or an aegis in her other hand. The "aegis of Bast" was a semi-circular shield adorned with the head of a lioness. This object betrayed her original role as a lioness-goddess.

She was the Goddess of Bubastis, a province of Lower Egypt, and around 950 B.C., when the city became the capitol of the kingdom, her statue was raised to that of a great national divinity. Bubastis means "the House of Bast," but as early as the fourth century B.C., she was considered to be supreme.

Bast, like Hathor, loved dancing and all kinds of merry-making. Using her sistrum, she would enhance the rhythm of the music, by adding the silvery, tinkling tones of the instrument. There were many festivals held in her honor all through the year and these were conducted in her own temple at Bubastis.

Bast's temple was one of the most elegant in Egypt and many thousands of people gathered there for the annual celebrations. They traveled by barge to the music of flutes, and a constant barrage of ribald good humor was exchanged between the travelers and the people on the banks of the great river, who gathered to watch the huge flotilla as it passed.

Bast was principally a goddess of pleasure and she was invoked with great merriment and the quaffing of much wine. It is said more wine was consumed at her festivals than at any other time during the year.

Most households had a consecrated statue of the goddess, and it was through the worship of Bast that cats became recognized as sacred animals. After death, they were carefully mummified and buried in the shadow of her sanctuaries.

Ra was the renowned sun-god of the Egyptians. His celebrated temple at Heliopolis was called Het Benben — "the Palace of the Obelisk" — and in the vast courtyard rose the obelisk of the Sun. There were many beautiful hymns sung there, composed by the Pharaoh himself. The songs glorified the Sun as creator and benefactor of the world.

The heretic pharaoh, Akhenaton, transformed Ra into Aten and proclaimed that all men were equally Children of Aten.

The Rite of Leo

After the Sun has entered the sign of Leo, choose a day which is truly hot and proceed to your circle. Give yourself plenty of time; there must be no sense of haste in this rite. Walk with a steady and determined tread and with a feeling of confidence and optimism.

With bare feet, enter, and circumambulate the ring clockwise, thinking of the previous signs that you have passed through. Make as many circuits as you deem necessary, then stand in the center, facing south.

Imagine the Celtic cross—the four equal arms surrounded by a circle. Raise your arms at your sides, palms facing the direction in which you are looking, feet together. Now, *you* are the cross within the circle and your heart is the center of this tiny universe that you have created. Think on this.

Now look "inward" and "see" your heart pumping the life-blood endlessly through all the veins and arteries of your body, even to the tips of your fingers and toes. This inner world is so strange when you attempt to visualize it. Usually, it is never thought about by the soul it carries through life. It is taken for granted, largely, and only if prompted will the mind answer the body's most urgent "messages." I need food; I need sleep; I need to evacuate waste material, etc., etc.

Pain is the warning the body gives you when something is wrong with it. When this occurs, some kind of painkiller is pushed into the body to keep it quiet and block the pain. The signal is virtually ignored, yet still persists, even though the drug temporarily has disconnected the brain from the nervous system. How *dare* we ignore these warnings from a structure that serves us so well? It would be wise to try and understand the messages when they arise, and especially *if they continue*. From this time forward, make up your mind to give due consideration to the body you inhabit.

Of course, human bodies, in the main, are capable of enduring any amount of ill-usage, and it is well for us that this is the case! But, in terms of general health, you will find that your concern will not go unrewarded, and you may even begin to feel extra vitality coursing through your limbs with any amount of energy at your disposal when you start to take care of yourself.

When ready, say:

"I dedicate my soul to the service of Light. I bless and purify this vehicle of Life, created by Love."

From a vial of perfumed oil, annoint your forehead, feet, hands (palms) and breasts.

"Blood is Light and Light is Life. May the spark of Divine Fire within grow in brightness and strength."

Renew the "cross" position and contemplate yourself as a living entity.

Lay down under the strong rays of the Sun; close your eyes and begin the visualization.

♌ ♌ ♌ ♌

The heat is intense and becoming stronger with every passing second. Your whole body is bathed in perspiration and you can see vivid flashes and shapes behind your closed eyes. You can bear the heat no longer and sit up wiping the moisture from your forehead with a bare arm. A hand placed carelessly on the sun-baked sand is withdrawn with a surprised yelp of pain—yes, it is *that* hot!

You are lying under a small group of palm trees in the desert, which stretches away from you—shimmering into the distance. A small pool lies under the trees, from which you thankfully drink. The silence beats upon your eardrums until an animal's low growl spins you round, and there, standing a little way off, is a magnificent lion. It turns its head to gaze at you; the great mane and pelt glistening like gold. Eyes, the color of deep amber and glowing like lamps, regard you benignly. It turns and lopes off and you know instinctively that you must follow it.

The white sand reflects the Sun's heat but you walk doggedly in the lion's tracks. It disappears over a sand dune and when you have gained the top of it, there, but a few feet away, rises a golden pyramid. Its apex is surmounted by a cone of sapphire and it shimmers in a faint mist of rainbow colors—it is magnificent!

As you approach, a robed and hooded figure can be seen standing in front of it. This is your guide.

The lion flops down in the shadow of the edifice and you follow the guide through a narrow entrance and into—utter blackness! You are given a robe of dark-blue velvet, then, by the flame of a small oil lamp, you are led into the heart of the pyramid.

After the hard brightness outside, it is as though you have been suddenly blinded. The small flame is all but overwhelmed by the stygian darkness and the only sound is that made by the movement of the robes.

The passages are very narrow and appear to continually change direction. Then, abruptly, you enter a chamber in which stands a large granite sarcophagus.

Your companion indicates the coffin, helps you into it, then departs. The words, "I will wait for you," flash into your mind, and you are comforted to know that you will not be abandoned in this place.

Now, even the small comfort of the flame has gone and the blackness is impenetrable. It makes not the slightest difference whether your eyes are open or closed! The air is quite fresh in the pyramid and the temperature is comfortable, being neither hot nor cold.

And so you wait, listening to the anxious thudding of your heart, and wondering.

Perhaps you slept? You are not sure, but somewhere, a long way off, a faint light is showing. Gradually, it comes nearer, or grows brighter, you cannot tell which. The light is very bright now, and out of it come two radiant forms—those of a man and a woman. They are resplendent in the dress and style of the ancient Egyptian gods. The man wears the crown of Upper and Lower Egypt, while the woman is adorned with the royal headdress, the Uraeus, upon her brow. You are in the presence of Isis and Osiris—the Queen of Heaven and her beloved Consort—two of the oldest deities in the universe.

Gently, they raise you, and with one on either side of you, escort you along an avenue of light which is composed of every shade of color you have known, and many that you have known not. It stretches far into the distance, and as you move along, you perceive two people coming towards you.

As they draw nearer, you recognize them. They are your mother and father! You hasten to greet them, your being filled with joy. Suddenly, you realize that you are once more a young child! Bewildered, you hold up small arms to your parents. They embrace you and kiss you, lovingly, then pass by. More people appear—familiar to you—your grandparents are here. They, too, greet you and pass on. People you do not recognize appear and pass by, until the horizon is filled with them! All are in the mode of dress they wore when living upon the Earth.

This mighty throng are your ancestors! Many have been reincarnated over the pages of history, but they are being presented to you now as the souls whose earthly bodies, over thousands of years, finally brought *you* into existence. These people are responsible for your *physical* body. Their blood runs in *your* veins—and some of their hereditary traits, too! *Yes, it has taken all of them to make you!* And amid them all, the forms of Isis and Osiris appear as wraiths; mingling and blending with them so that every man and woman seems to issue and emanate through them.

Eventually, the vision fades, and the God and Goddess take your hands, and the words come.

"We are your primal parents—the great forces of polarity through which life is manifested. We appear in a guise that is pleasing and recognizable to you, and one which was of a race in touch with truth and beauty. Therefore, know that as you once were, you yet shall be, even to eternity. Though the body is finite, the Blood Royal comes from what we are and is ever present. From the source of life, it is indestructible, being the Father of the Sun and the Mother of the Moon."

Together, the three of you walk back along the Avenue of Light until you are floating above the sarcophagus, which glows, faintly, in the darkness of the pyramid. The God and Goddess lower you very gently into it, one on either side, and watch over you, their hands spread out in a benediction. Then Isis and Osiris are drawn back into the light, which slowly dissolves into nothingness.

Your guide comes quickly and makes some rapid passes over you. It is time to leave. Very soon you can see a small rectangle of daylight—the entrance to the pyramid. Your robe is taken from you and, with hands pressed against your eyes, you emerge once more into the glaring brightness of the desert.

The lion comes to you, and without any fear you place a hand on the thick mane and allow the animal to guide you back to the oasis. Gratefully, you both drink from the pool, then, with the King of the Beasts settling at your feet, you lean against a palm tree and close your eyes.

When you open them, you are within your circle. Relax your mind and slowly adjust to your surroundings. Take your time and partake of some refreshment. The sun is lower in the sky and has lost its intense heat. A faint breeze is blowing—which somehow reminds you of the Avenue of Light. Before leaving, raise your hands, palms outward, towards the Sun, the representative of the Solar Logos, and say: "May Aten's light be ever with me—even to Eternity!"

VIRGO

AUGUST 23RD–SEPTEMBER 22ND

Planet: Mercury

Jewel: Blue Sapphire

Number: 5

Governs: Intestines,
Nervous system

Color: Silver-gray

Metal: Platinum

Flower: Morning Glory

Herb: Fennel

Positive Traits

Discriminating; modest; tidy; analytical; meticulous.

Negative Traits

Fussy; a worrier; hypercritical; unreliable; falsely modest; pedantic.

VIRGO

The high turning castle in the North,
the aeons-old chalk roads.
The star-teller on the plains,
the sword-smithy on the downs.
The silver voice near-silent from the earth,
the Virgin Lady, shimmering, on the edge of mind,
white, through the branches, by the stream:
In this land as for wider,
from the tiding of the seas
to the rising of the Pleiades.
From Atlantis to the Magellanics,
in grace, the star-clothed rules.

PETER BURFORD-WOOD

VIRGO

Virgo is the second earth sign and the second mutable sign of the zodiac. Its beautiful symbol is that of the Virgin, or maiden, holding a sheaf of wheat in her hand. Virgo symbolizes harvest time, yet the figure is winged and the sign is ruled by Mercury, the Lord of Air. Thus, it encompasses nourishment for the soul as well as the body.

This sign is the alchemist of the zodiac, differentiating spirit and matter and refining them in the crucible of life. Virgo is the sign of purity, so that which is sought is the end product produced by sifting the wheat from the chaff, so to speak. Nothing less than that tiny nugget of gold is acceptable to the soul in Virgo.

Perfection and accuracy are aimed at when shaping metals or carving wood into artifacts. This soul takes the products of the earth and molds them into fine works of art. The mind is careful and detailed, following the harmony of creation as seen in the humblest flower or plant. The influence here is one of mental agility— comparing, analyzing and criticizing.

Virgo is much concerned with hygiene and matters of health, and is aware that disease can spring from selfish thoughts, fear, or apprehension. Therefore, the maiden infuses the soul with a desire for this cleanliness and purity. The soul must then guide the mind and the mind must control the body so that there is a clear run-through of illuminating and healing light.

There is an important link, here, between the Greek goddess, Hygeia, and the Maiden of the Mysteries—the Virgin. Long have the mysteries informed that a contented mind breeds a healthy body, a truth known to initiates of most traditions.

This is the last of the six physical signs referring to Self-hood and to the development of the personality. Seeing the Self as the center of things ends in the sign of Virgo.

In this sign, the soul begins to understand that matter is not what it appears, *i.e.*, solid! So, in Virgo, two things happen. Matter is broken down and found to be composed of atoms and energy—not solid at all. And the Self perceives, however dimly, that at some stage in the future the personality or persona must be controlled by the intellect and not allowed to continue indefinitely as "top dog!" The persona must be refined and filled with particles of light from the spirit, so that it shines for all to see, and becomes, in actuality, a true reflection of the Higher Self.

This is the sign of science, and Mercury draws these children of earth to investigate everything with which they come into contact. Small slivers of life are taken and subjected to microscopic analysis—to see what makes things tick! In a young soul, this type of thinking is taken to extremes, until the obsession with trivialities causes many a rift in associations.

The mind is almost closed to the wider issues of life because the soul is enmeshed in its own world of minutiae. If this is allowed to continue, there will be confusion and misunderstanding. Everything the young soul sees as a victory will be viewed by others as the logical solution to an everyday problem—encountered then dismissed. Any arrogance will be treated with an unbelieving stare, which in the words of a famous tennis star, means, "Man, you cannot be serious!"

The Virgo soul scrutinizes anything it considers worthy of scrutiny. Occult subjects are taken apart with cold precision. This may be all very admirable when seeking truth, but the danger here lies in attempting to dissect things of a spiritual nature which virtually refuse to be dissected. Belonging, as they do, to a different order of consciousness, they must be recognized as such, and approached through methods of meditation or ritual. A young soul can be severely limited in its spiritual progress simply because it is exploring the mystical in a scientific manner. In some cases, there is a refusal to admit the existence of anything beyond the physical.

The advanced soul working in Virgo understands that the maiden is the mediator, the bridge between the seen and the unseen. Her beautiful wings represent the spiritual working through matter. She is the guardian of the divine spark—that spark which *inspires* matter. The sign of Virgo contains the secret of the mystery of life, and in the zodiac, Virgo merges the physical signs with the six successive spiritual ones.

No better illustration of the meaning of Virgo could be included here than the doctrine of the legendary Hermes Trismegistus (thrice-greatest Hermes), or Thoth, the Egyptian god of knowledge. Under his Roman name of Mercury, he is, of course, the ruler of this sign.

The doctrine is said to have been engraved upon the Smaragden, or Emerald tablet, and is a synthesis on the mystery of life, an acknowledged key to alchemy and the foundation of astrology and magic. It is given here in its entirety.

It is true!
It is sure!
It is the full truth!
That which is below
is like to that which is above,

and that which is above
is like to that which is below
so that the wonders of the One are enacted.

• • •

And as all things have been and come into
being from the One, through one mediator, so
are they all born from this one Marriage by
adaptation.

• • •

The father of it is the Sun,
The mother is the Moon.

• • •

The Wind has carried it in his womb,
the Earth is the wet nurse.
The father of all perfection
of all the world is here.

• • •

Its force is entire if it is turned into earth.

• • •

You shall, softly and with great insight,
separate the Earth from the Fire,
the subtle from the gross.
It rises from the Earth to the sky
and again descends to the Earth,
so taking to it the force
from that which is above
and that which is below.

• • •

So shall you own the glory
of the whole world and
therefore shall all darkness flee from you.

• • •

This is the powerful strength of all strengths,
for it shall vanquish anything subtle,
and anything solid penetrate.

• • •

Thus is the world created.

• • •

From this shall, in the same way,
wonderful adaptations be created.

• • •

Therefore have I been called
thrice-great Hermes because I possess
the three aspects of the Wisdom's
doctrine of the whole world.

• • •

What I have said about the preparation of gold,
the operation of the Spiritual Sun, is finished.

• • •

This sign is called the "Hidden Fire of the Earth."
Virgo symbolizes purification.

Legends

Of the Virgin

The Egyptian Isis was a virgin-mother and was shown with her divine son, Horus, at her breast. In many statues, she was portrayed naked—as was her son. But, in the Mysteries of Egypt she was always veiled—an obvious symbol of her chastity. "Immaculate is our Lady Isis," is the legend engraved upon a carving of Serapis and Isis.

The Virgin Mary succeeded to the attributes which were formerly given to Isis. These included symbols, titles, ceremonies, and festivals, with the new priesthood observing the rules of the previous religion. These included a vow of celibacy, a compulsory tonsure and the wearing of the surplice.

Statues of the Virgin are virtually identical in detail to those of Isis; particularly where the Virgin is represented as the Queen of Heaven and is seated on the crescent moon, symbol of virginity. Isis and other pagan goddesses also had similar titles, such as Queen of Heaven, Queen of the Universe, Mother of God, the Celestial Virgin, and so on.

In a Yugoslavian psalter, the Virgin and child are seated in a black boat, echoing the Moon-boat of the Great Goddess, while in a Flemish manuscript, the Virgin is shown embracing the zodiac and the planetary sphere.

A painting from Germany c. 1400 discloses the Virgin Mary engaged in the domestic work of spinning. A thread in her hands runs through her body to the place where the Christ child is developing in her womb. The ancient Goddess was often pictured as the spinning goddess of destiny, especially in her three-fold aspect of the Fates. Whether intentionally or otherwise, the artist of the painting has re-created the same qualities of the feminine principle, namely those of creating life.

Black Isis has been transformed into the Black Virgin, which in France has proved to be actual basalt figures of Isis! The special veneration in which the Black Virgin is held reveals an esteemed and ancient lineage.

One of the most blatant "borrowings" from the goddess religion is the Christian nativity scene. From Neolithic times, the Goddess as Lady of the Mountain and Mistress of the Animals, was worshipped in a byre, with her animals around her. For was she not also revered as the Holy Cow? And were not kings and priests nourished on her milk? An Assyrian text[6] attests this truth:

> Little was thou, Assurbanipal, when I
>   delivered
> thee to the Queen of Nineveh,
> Weak wast thou, when thou didst sit upon her
>   knees,
> Four teats were set in thy mouth.

A statue of the Goddess, or a symbol denoting her presence, was placed before the byre. Notable was the existence of the downward-pointing triangle and the reed-bundle. The latter was a device which would be let down over the entrance to keep the animals contained and, assuredly, was the chief symbol of the Goddess as the Gate. The entire sanctuary was thought of as her body and betokened her presence.

Greek

The Virgin aspect of the Goddess was enacted by Artemis, Apollo's sister. When she was but a little girl,

---

[6]This text is from stone tablets found in the library of the great Assyrian Emperor, Assurbanipal, in Nineveh, 7th century B.C.

she asked Zeus, her father, if she could have (among other things) the gift of eternal virginity, a bow and arrow, the office of bringing light, a saffron hunting dress with a red hem, and sixty young ocean nymphs of the same age to be her companions. She said that she intended to live in the mountains of the world, and like her mother, Leto, to be patroness of childbirth. Zeus granted all her wishes, and more beside.

The Maiden Huntress of the Silver Bow, or crescent moon, was the youngest in the trinity of the Moon-Goddess. And many of the priestesses of Artemis would daub their faces with white clay in her honor. This goddess had a great statue erected in her name at Athens which was known as "the white-browed."

Her title, Lady of the Wild Things, denotes her affinity with animals, but her legendary hunting of them speaks of a hardness in her character not noticeable in other aspects of the goddess, three-fold. Then, too, Artemis had the power to send all manner of plagues upon mankind. She could ordain sudden death or a quick recovery from illness, and was, like her symbol the Moon, extremely changeable in her moods.

Artemis was offered a host of animals and birds to be sacrificed annually in her honor, and this custom survived into classical times at Patrae, a city of Calydonia. At Hierapolis, the victims were hung on trees in an artificial forest within her temple.

Celtic

The goddess Brigid, or Bride, was the Celtic Virgin. She was known as the Maiden Goddess of Purity—the chaste maiden of the snows. Her festival was celebrated on February 2nd, amid the depths of winter. The snow-drop became Bride's symbol, being the first white flower to emerge above the frozen earth. As an expert in poetry, learning, divination and healing, the goddess was held in great reverence, and, on the eve of her festival, the following custom took place.

A sheaf of wheat was dressed in a white gown, to depict the goddess, and laid in a basket or crib which was called Bride's bed. A phallic-shaped rod or club was then placed beside the goddess and the women of the house would say, "Bride is come, Bride is most welcome!" These words were repeated three times as three candles were lit, then left beside the bed to burn throughout the night. The following day, a virgin of the house, or the youngest female, would come into the room and examine the ashes in the hearth. If the outline of a rod was seen it was taken as a sign that the year to come would be a lucky one with a bountiful harvest.

Christian

With the advent of Christianity, the goddess Bride was replaced by St. Brigid. She was born, it is said, at sunrise, neither within nor outside a house; was fed from the milk of a white, red-eared cow, and hung her wet cloak on the rays of the sun. The house where she stayed appeared to be ablaze with light. She and nineteen of her nuns took turns to guard a sacred fire which burned perpetually and was enclosed by a hedge where no male could enter.

St. Brigid is said to have lived around A.D. 453–523. Her great monastery at Kildare was most probably built on an ancient sanctuary dedicated to the Celtic Virgin. One legend speaks of her marriage to Bres, son of a Fomarian father, whose mother came from the Tuatha De' Danann, the children of Dana. But her role is very similar to the goddess whom she superseded in that her function was to breed, and to keep the home fires burning.

Roman

Vesta was a Roman goddess of virginity and purity and was likened to the everlasting flame which graced her temples. The idea of shining purity is also suggested in her name which was derived from the Sanskrit root, *vas*, meaning clear and pure.

Like other virgin goddesses, Vesta also represented motherhood, and what appears to be a contradiction in terms stems from the ancient idea of a divine son being born of a virgin. The concept of the Immaculate Conception was part of the mysteries of the goddess and predates the Christian religion. There was a definite method incorporated here that involved both the mystical and the mundane and one which ensured that the Virgin Priestess remained a virgin.

The reason behind this mystery was the idea of bringing to birth an "old soul" or teacher, to lead the race forward and to instruct the priesthood in both spiritual and temporal matters.

There were sixteen savior gods before Jesus, with almost identical stories. One of them was Bel, a Babylonian god, who lived nearly 2,000 years earlier. Inscriptions on stone were found in Babylon and stated that Bel was taken prisoner, was tried in the Hall of Justice, was scourged and then led away to the mount. With him were two thieves, one of whom was released. After his execution the city broke out in tumult. His clothes were carried away and he went down into the mount and disappeared from life. A weeping woman saw him at the gate of burial. He was brought back to life.

Vesta was worshipped in private as well as in the public sphere, and all households had their individual shrines where a flame always burned. The home fire, and those who tend it, is said to be the most sacred of all the paths, as it represents the life of the race which it nourishes and cradles. Vesta's chief festival was celebrated on June 7th, but she was also honored throughout the year.

Pure water was offered to her in clay vases. These were very narrow at the base so that they would not stand upon the ground. The Goddess was served by priestesses called the vestal virgins, and none but they were admitted into the Great One's presence, unless a formal festival occurred.

The vestals were drawn from patrician families and were chosen by lot. They entered a college between the ages of 6 and 10 years and took vows of complete chastity. They usually remained in the service of the Goddess for thirty years. Their initial service included learning their duties and becoming initiated into the Mysteries of the Goddess. Vestals who broke their vows were put to death. In early times, this involved being scourged to death, and at a later date, extended to being scourged and walled-up alive in a suitable tomb.

One of the most important duties of a vestal was to keep the sacred fire alight. If it went out, the guilty female was put to death by whipping, publicly, in the Forum Boarium. It was therefore understandable that a mere twenty vestals broke their vows in the course of eleven centuries!

Their privileges, however, were many, and included being honored when they appeared in public always preceded by a lictor. At the end of their term of office, they were at liberty to marry, but many preferred to continue in the manner to which they had become accustomed. One interesting tradition states that if a condemned man happened upon a vestal he was unconditionally given his freedom.

The Rite of Virgo

When the Sun has entered the sign of the Virgin, you may enact the rite. A flame must be taken from a fire in your home, and carried to the site. Virgoan ingenuity will be required here, but it *is* possible!

Arriving at your destination, place the flame in the center of the circle and begin with a period of contemplation upon the following theme:

How have these rites affected you up to now?

Have you noticed an improvement in your physical, mental or emotional states of being?

Do you feel any significant change has occurred, either in yourself, or in the way you view the world?

This is the time for an assessment of your experiences so far. So, armed with writing materials, start by answering the above questions and any others you feel are appropriate at this time.

An important feature of esoteric philosophy is the idea that everything in the universe is interconnected. Harmonies and vibrations thrill through it and all life is part of the whole. Each living organism has its appointed place in the scheme of things, and the Tree of Life, a symbol of this cosmic plan, is an excellent representation.

The animal kingdom moves through the impulses imposed upon it by the lunar forces, but human beings are placed higher on the Tree of Life. As such, you have been endowed with mental qualities which allow you to decide what you *will become*. In other words, you have freewill and the charge of the physical vehicle that you inhabit. You, and only you, are its keeper and its guardian.

But, would it not be easier to forget the whole idea of initiation and drift with the next idle thought or new fancy which presents itself? Of course it would! That is the easy way out! Most people find their pleasures or distractions in everyday activities and do not look beyond the gratification of one of their five senses. Would you be as they? Or does such a lifestyle find you discontented with the ordinary, the mundane? Is there an emptiness—a void—which leaves your spirit unfulfilled? And is *that* the reason why you are reading this book?

When you have concluded the assessment of Self, make ready for the rite. Light some incense of a suitable aroma and carry it round the circle. Allow your thoughts to quieten. Breathe deeply and become *en rapport* with the character of the sign. Then place the incense beside the flame and declaim:

"Now, the Light of the World stands in Virgo— the last of the physical signs. It gives me the opportunity to build a bridge towards the following six signs which speak of the spirit. I will grow, as a tree, firmly grounded on the Earth which gave me birth. My limbs, like branches, wield the implements I use in life-learning and carry me on the bosom of the Earth Mother. I am here to seek knowledge through investigation which will lead to Wisdom in Service."

Having made sure that your body will be warm and comfortable during the visualization, lay down and close your eyes.

♍ ♍ ♍ ♍

The air is dank in your nostrils and there is moisture dripping from somewhere above. Opening your astral eyes, you find yourself in what appears to be an underground passage. The walls gleam with wetness and the edges of many diverse minerals show in the faint light. The dark green of malachite, the reddish-brown of carnelian and the many pastel colors of quartz.

You start to walk carefully along in the semi-darkness—wondering. After a while, the passage suddenly opens into a large cave. At your feet, a yawning abyss descends into nothingness. You shiver in the chilly atmosphere.

As your eyes become a little more accustomed to the gloom, you notice that this place has a definite shape. That of the *vesica pisces*—the elongated oval of the Great Mother. A narrow bridge leads to the other side of the chasm. It is constructed from gold and silver ropes, plaited together, with rough-hewn planks of wood to walk upon. It sways slightly from time to time when an occasional rush of wind sweeps through the cave from another passage beyond the bridge. It would seem that this is the route you must take if you are to continue your journey!

With great trepidation you place a foot upon the first plank, your hands gripping the ropes. The bridge trembles and moves alarmingly—the black gulf beneath awaiting your slightest error. Very slowly, you take another step, then another, your hands, wet with perspiration, sliding over the glittering cords.

Step by tortuous step, you make your way across; the currents of icy wind whipping past, to rush, moaning, through the tunnel behind you. It seems an eternity before you step upon the final plank—and you are safely across the void.

You stand a moment to recover from the ordeal and glance back into the cave. The bridge is alive with light, flashing a myriad rainbow colors into the darkness.

The passage climbs slowly upwards and you notice the roots of trees crossing the floor and roof of the tunnel, revealing that their life-giving structure spreads deep underground.

You emerge into a great forest filled with golden light. Leaves, fluttering to the ground, speak of early Autumn. Animals scamper in the undergrowth and the notes of songbirds rise, in a peaon of praise.

You follow a path through the trees and remember the hidden life of the strong roots taking sustenance from the Earth Mother. The path leads to a glade where a stone circle stands on a carpet of smooth turf. A small fire burns brightly in the center of the stones, and you walk over to it and enter the ring.

On a slab of rock you find a lump of clay and a bowl of water. Begin to mold the clay. It matters not what form it takes, but try to do it to the best of your ability. You may find the clay taking shape under your fingers, without any conscious effort of thought. When you have finished, leave the result of your labor upon the rock, as an offering to the gods, and continue the journey.

The sound of muffled hoofbeats momentarily startles you into taking shelter behind some bushes. A flash of white shows through the golden leaves and a milk-white unicorn charges into view, mane and tail flying. It halts abruptly a few feet away, the golden hoofs scattering the fallen leaves. The magical creature rears up, neighing proudly, its slender legs combing the air; then stands, ears pricked, head turned in your direction.

Summoning courage again, you approach the beautiful animal. It tosses its head impatiently, and the gilded horn flashes in the sun's rays. A fallen log makes a convenient foothold and you scramble onto the broad back.

The unicorn moves off immediately, carrying you deeper into the forest. Hands clutching the silken mane, you feel the great muscles rippling beneath you—the animal's coat, satin-smooth to your touch. Too soon, the unicorn pauses in a broad avenue and you slide to the ground. The soft muzzle gently pushes at your back, so you walk into the clearing, the fabulous beast following.

Tall trees guard this place, their branches mingling above your head. With each step the light becomes more brilliant—the foliage luminous and aflame. Sounds of mellifluous harmonies fill the air—throbbing and undulating—faint at first, then swelling with the light and reverberating through the forest.

You are witnessing the manifestation of cosmic harmony—that which keeps the stars in their courses and governs the universe. It dazzles, and all but overcomes you.

The avenue leads to a huge circular glade where the light coalesces into a single column at the center. The music is absorbed by this column of light and is transformed into a single bell-tone of unutterable sweetness. Your limbs tremble and your skin crawls with a fearful awe at the majesty laid before you. A reaction felt when a god passes by. And, now, you are possessed of such bliss that you *will* to be "at one" with the wonderful vision, although it is extremely difficult to gaze upon.

Something touches your shoulder, and turning, you see Mercury standing there.

"I am pleased that you have come this far," he says, smiling. You turn away, confused.

"I know how you feel, but surely this is what you came to discover?" He indicates the radiance.

You smile at him, apologetically. Mercury's clear gray eyes hold yours and you know that he understands your feelings very well indeed.

"Look!" He draws a sigil in the air and the column of light becomes transparent, revealing a marvelous tree at its center.

As you watch, entranced, blossoms burst forth, bloom, then fall, to be replaced by others in a miraculous dance.

"It is the Tree of Life. It permeates all the planes of existence and states of being, as the physical plane is only one of many. What you have just experienced will work like leaven and create a stronger link between your soul and its source. During incarnation in matter, the soul may be dimly aware of its origins, but people often deny its existence because they are enmeshed in the material world.

"The sign of Virgo speaks of an alchemical change which must always come from within. You have witnessed the secret formulae of transformation—the spark of divine energy that permeates the entire universe; the life force that is immortal and can never be destroyed. With this knowledge, you will go forward revitalized, your spirit illuminated and your features glowing from the radiance within. Your body will be stronger as the molecules are thus energized. And now, I will leave you with the Lady. Until we meet again, Farewell!"

Mercury soars into the column of light and is gone, but standing in his place is a lovely young woman! Her gown shimmers, as snow on a frosty morning, and her face shines with an unearthly light. She holds out her hand and leads you away from the glade. Glancing back, you see the unicorn at rest near the Tree of Life, and you send out a special thought to him.

Quite soon, the Lady opens a door in the stout bark of a large oak tree, revealing a flight of steps which descend into the bowels of the earth. At the bottom, you find you are in the passage from whence you began this journey. And there, your head cradled in the Lady's soft lap, the scene slowly fades.

In the environment of your circle, as always, take time to adjust to the physical world. Renew the incense and partake of some refreshments. When ready stand in the center of the circle and say:

"I have kept my troth, and give thanks to the Gods and the Dwellers on the inner Planes. I leave this place a wiser and more enlightened soul, at peace with the universe and eager to continue on the path. I will follow the Sun through the zodiac, and as each sign is illuminated, I will seek to discover its inner meanings and its message. At each station, a new adventure and a cosmic truth, revealed.

"O' thou Girdle of Venus, shining in the vault of Heaven, in truth thou art a beacon to the aspiring soul. (Raise arms to sky.) Where thou art, I yet shall be, through thine illumination!"

The following rites are performed indoors, but the circle should be visited at least once a month, in order to maintain your magical link with both the place and your previous experiences.

Make a silent promise to return, then collect your belongings and depart.

LIBRA

SEPTEMBER 23RD–OCTOBER 22ND

Planet: Venus
Jewel: Opal
Number: 6
Governs: Kidneys

Color: Lavender
Metal: Copper
Flower: Red Rose
Herb: Yarrow

Positive Traits
Charming; romantic; diplomatic; refined; aesthetic;
idealistic.

Negative Traits
Indecisive; frivolous; gullible; flirtatious.

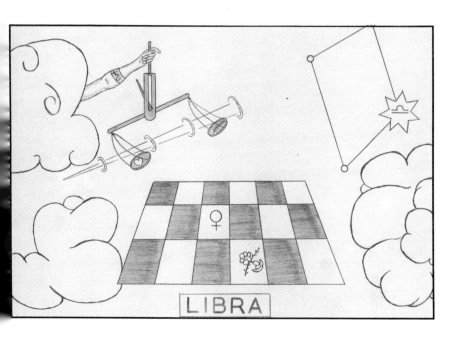

LIBRA

The Scales of the Equinox hang in the air,
keeping the Balance of old:
When daytime and nighttime are equal,
and Summer to Winter is sold.
Venus, the ruler of Cardinal Air,
gives beauty and gentle demean;
Lover of Justice, avenger of wrongs,
the Zodiac's Law-giving Queen.
First in the six of the spiritual signs,
holding the balance of twelve;
Betwix'st light and dark, the body and soul,
in regeneration to delve.
The Aula of Venus—a mystery here
of love and its highest ideal;
Expressed by the Scales and the blending of both,
with Marriage its manifest seal.

PATRICIA C. CROWTHER

LIBRA

Libra is the second air sign and the third cardinal sign of the zodiac and is represented by the symbol of the scales. Here, at the gate of Autumn, when day and night are equal, the Scales of Justice hang in perfect equilibrium.

Venus, the goddess of love and beauty, leads the way into the next six signs, as the Sun begins its return journey through the second half of the zodiac.

A more ancient and profound symbol of Libra is the Aula, or Altar of Venus. Originally, this was the body of woman and a female would become the "altar" when the mysteries were performed. As a life-giving vessel, woman was considered to be the Goddess, incarnate, and as such, was given due reverence.

As the second of the air signs, Libra introduces abstract thought and the motivation is usually through this element in its active or cardinal phase. The energy in Libra is refined and poised, the mental processes working to maintain the balance and harmony of the sign.

Instinctively, there is a dislike of argument and often a refusal to take one side or the other, even though the soul recognizes the rights and wrongs of a situation. This, of course, can be infuriating! It often results in compromise, which *can* be viewed as weakness.

The influence of Venus bestows an intense desire for peace and a natural instinct for "pouring oil on troubled waters." The soul yearns for tranquil conditions. It can feel physically ill if placed in a hostile atmosphere, or where there is constant bickering and disharmony.

This is the sign of marriage and partnership, so there is no desire to live alone. And although the soul is contented when working with, or through others, the nerves will be stretched to the breaking point at the least sign of discord or dissension. A completely harmonious love match is essential for the soul in Libra, and this is often attained to a degree rarely achieved by other signs.

Because this sign is happiest in beautiful and elegant surroundings, it has earned the epithet "Lazy Libra." This is an unfair comment as most Librans are extremely clever and work hard in their professions. They desire perfection and strive for it in all they do, being very conscientious workers, indeed.

As an active air sign, their perception of beauty is truly aesthetic and their homes are usually tastefully decorated with fine pieces of porcelain and objects d'art.

Libra is profoundly artistic and many of these souls are fine musicians, singers or actors. The sign is creative, and under the rulership of Venus many works of art come from the pen or paintbrush of the Libran.

The sensitivity is very great and in some souls is acute to the point of pain. To them, a slight, or careless remark, will deeply wound and be remembered long afterwards.

Young souls working in Libra often appear to be lacking in emotional warmth because, at the least sign of disharmony, they will gravitate to another more comfortable environment, without any apparent lack of conscience. Thus, they are often accused of disloyalty. This longing for the sweet life can be a big stumbling block to their advancement. The lesson here is to direct the needs of the Self towards others. When this has been learned, the true qualities of gentleness and tact can work in all kinds of situations.

Since perception is razor-sharp, this sign of justice will bring equity and balance to all areas of human relationships. And with the harmonious vibrations from Venus, the high ideals of cosmic reciprocity incorporated here will find a perfect channel for expression.

The advanced soul will strive for equality and fairness in all decisions and matters which come under its jurisdiction. Law and liberty are its very life-blood, and where it sees injustice it will fight on a mental level, with all the eloquence at its command, in order to remedy the position. All actions, in this respect, will be totally dispassionate, no matter how bitter the recriminations. The advanced soul's vision is developed far beyond the prejudices and opinions of the masses.

Libra is intimately linked with the Law of Karma, and many souls will encounter a life where karmic debts have to be discharged. The planet Saturn is exalted in Libra, and Saturn has much to do with the law of cause and effect. The scales must balance in perfect equilibrium before the soul can continue its journey.

Often, there will occur the opportunity to defend an unusual belief or philosophy which has lain forgotten or has been an object of ridicule or derision. The soul brings all the weight of a fine analytical mind and a clear-cut vision to bear in discussion and debate, so that the pure light of truth emerges and once again the scales are balanced.

As diplomat and arbitrator, it is poised, like the Ape of Thoth, in the center of the scales. It follows the middle way, holds the balance between all opposites, and upholds the light of spiritual truth and justice. This sign is known as the "Earthly Paradise." *Libra represents cosmic love, law and harmony.*

Legends

Greek

After Metis (Wisdom), Zeus married Themis, daughter of Uranus and Gaea. Themis was the law-giver and represented both physical and moral order. Her children were Horae, or Seasons, Eunomia (Wise Legislation), Eirene (Peace), Dike (Justice) and the Fates or Morerae.

Although Themis was put aside for Hera, she was always at the side of Zeus as his advisor, and continued to be revered on Olympus.

Themis was the most important of the Lesser Gods. Her mission was to maintain order and regulate all ceremonies. She, it was, who invited the gods to meetings and prepared their banquets.

Themis was the goddess of Justice and her province also included the Earth. She was protectress of the just and punisher of the guilty, hence her epithet, *Soteir Soteira*. Themis was also called Euboulos, the good counsellor, and as Goddess of Wisdom she advised the judges in their verdicts. She possessed the gift of prophecy and it is said that she once owned Delphi.

It was to Delphi that Deucalion, the son of Prometheus, and his wife, Pyrrha, journeyed in order to pray to Themis. Zeus had sent a deluge to annihilate the human race, but, being warned of this by his father, Deucalion built an ark. They floated on the waters for nine days and nights, then disembarked on Mount Parnassus.

Arriving at Delphi, they prayed to the goddess to save the human race. Themis appeared before them and said "Veil your heads! Remove the girdles of your robes and cast behind you the bones of your first ancestor."

After some thought, Deucalion and Pyrrha solved this enigmatic command. They covered their heads and walking across the valley, threw stones over their shoulders. Their reasoning was that as they were descendants of Gaea, the Earth Mother, the stones must be her very bones! The stones thrown by Deucalion were miraculously changed into men, while those cast by Pyrrha became transformed into women.

Temples in honor of Themis were erected throughout Greece at such places as Athens, Troezen, Thebes and Olympia. She was portrayed as a woman of austere appearance, carrying a pair of scales.

Babylonian

Shamash was the Babylonian Sun-god and sprang out of the Mountain of the East every morning. Swiftly, he climbed to the top of the mountain and there joined Bunene, his coachman. Bunene prepared the chariot of the god, who took his place therein.

In a blaze of light, Shamash climbed ever higher into the sky and in the evening brought his chariot to the great Mountain of the West. The Sun-god traveled through the dark subterranean tunnels of the earth and emerged once more from the Mountain of the East.

Shamash was a god of great vitality and courage. Did he not put the winter to flight and triumph over the darkness? His chief function, however, was as a god of Justice. His light searched out the evil-doer and penetrated the shadows where criminals might hide. It was said that he "breaks the horn of him who meditates evil." As light overcomes darkness, so did Shamash bring to justice those who committed iniquities. Some of his titles were: Judge of the Heavens and the Earth, Sublime Judge of the Anunnaki, and Lord of Judgment.

His temple in Babylon was named the House of the Judge of the World. Shamash was represented, seated on his throne, holding a scepter and a ring.

The Sun-god has another important role—that of the God of Divination. He would reveal the future through the *baru* or soothsayer. Having made a sacrifice to the god, the *baru* would pour oil on the water in the sacred cauldron and then observe the patterns and shapes that the oil made. Being an adept in both astronomy and astrology, the soothsayer would also interpret the movements of the stars and planets to foretell the future, under the direction of Shamash.

The art of divination was extremely popular at Sippar, where both Shamash and his wife, Aya, received great veneration. The divine couple became the parents of two gods who epitomized the abstract qualities of the Sun-god: Kittu—Justice, and Misharu—Law.

Egyptian
In Ancient Egypt, Maat was the goddess of Law, Truth and Justice. She wore an ostrich feather as a headdress which was the ideogram of her name. Maat was the beloved daughter and confidante of Ra, and wife to Thoth. She played a part of supreme importance in the Judgment of the Dead and the ceremony of Weighing the soul. This took place in a hall of immense proportions called the Hall of Double Maati, or the Hall of Double Justice. And Maat was doubled into two identical goddesses who guarded one end of this vast room.

Across its great length, she faced Osiris and Isis who stood in a shrine guarded by the divine uraeus, or asp. Down each side sat the forty-two gods known as the Assessors. These latter beings represented various aspects of the dead person's conscience. They were arrayed in winding sheets, and each carried a sharp-edged sword in his hand.

The center of the hall was occupied by a dais upon which stood an enormous pair of golden scales. Over all this awesome scene there fell a shaft of brilliant white light which negated any shadow, being the Light of Truth, itself.

The deceased stood before Osiris, arrayed in white with hands raised in adoration. He, or she, addressed the god with the obligatory Hymn of Praise, then speaking to the forty-two gods, would utter what was known as the Negative Confession.

The actual weighing of the heart was performed by the jackal-headed god, Anubis. Sometimes, Maat sat in one of the vast pans, or conversely, her feather was placed therein.

Anubis duly noted and recorded the weight of the heart, then announced it to Osiris. If the scales were in perfect equilibrium, the god declaimed accordingly: "Let the deceased depart victorious. Let him go wherever he wishes to mingle freely with the gods and the spirits of the dead." But if the heart failed to balance with the Feather of Truth it was immediately eaten by Amemait, the Devourer, a monster, part-crocodile, part-lion, which crouched near the scales.

Miscellaneous
In Babylon, the constellation of Libra was associated with the judgment of the living and the dead, and Zibanitu, the Scales, weighed the souls.

• • •

In Egypt, the harvest was weighed when the Moon was full in Libra.

• • •

The Greeks considered that the Balance was placed among the stars to perpetuate the memory of Mochus, the inventor of weights and measures.

• • •

The poet, Virgil, spoke of Libra, thus:

But when Astrae's balance hung on high,
Betwixt the nights and days divides the sky,
Then yoke your oxen, sow your winter grain,
Till cold December comes with driving rain.[7]

The Rite of Libra

We have passed through the initial six signs of the zodiac, and when the Sun illuminates Libra at the Autumn Equinox, the following six journeys will begin.

Each of these succeeding signs can best be described as the higher octaves of the previous ones. Blending the *body* of the initial six, with the *spirit* of the following six. And the twelve signs, in order of sequence, express steps in the evolutionary process. Situated at the midpoint of the zodiac, Libra reveals that the body is indeed the House of the Soul.

A table, to become an altar, must be dedicated to your work and set apart from mundane objects. A smooth, polished surface looks pleasing to the eye, and upon it should reside, at all times, a vase of fresh flowers.

When the Sun has entered Libra, consecrate the altar by placing lighted incense under it. The fragrant smoke will permeate the wood and rise to enclose the surface, thereby wholly purifying it. Scented oil of a

---

[7]Virgil, quoted by Mary Proctor in *Evenings with the Stars* (London: Cassell & Co., 1924), p. 87.

similar perfume can be lightly smeared around its edges, or underneath its surface.

While the Rite is in progress, a candle should be burning upon the altar, in the color attributed to the sign in which you are working. A symbol or picture of the sign should also be displayed to remind you of its content. But, apart from the above items, i.e., flowers, candle and sign, the altar should remain as uncluttered as possible.

When you purify and dedicate the altar, make a formal address of your intentions and what you *will* to accomplish or become, speaking from the heart.

When all is ready, light the candle and sit down in a comfortable chair. This rite begins with a period of contemplation along the following lines:

Allow your gaze to dwell upon the altar, and try to realize how long it has taken this piece of furniture to become what you see before you. From a tiny seed, it quickened in the earth, then pushed small shoots towards the light. It spent long years growing into a sapling, until the roots, searching underground for nourishment, spread wider still, mirroring the branches reaching to the Sun.

The first leaves, tender and bright green, bursting forth and rustling with movement. Birds, building nests and chirping contentedly in the tree's foliage. More years, gaining maturity, until you were born, and still more. A great giant at last, standing with others of its kin, and all performing a miracle. That of taking in carbon dioxide and giving out life-giving oxygen for the world and its inhabitants.

At last, the whining saw, severing the tree from the Earth Mother; its long life in the sun and air at an end. But still, the molecules of the wood remain, and skillful hands achieve a transformation. The elemental life of the tree has departed, but a new beauty is achieved, and once again, the tree is of service to humanity. Think on all this.

Now, prepare for the visualization. Look just above the candle-flame for a while, then close your eyes on the World of Form.

≏   ≏   ≏   ≏

When your inner eyes open, the light is still there. It is the light of a Full Moon and the orb bathes everything in a silvery radiance—it is almost as bright as day!

You are sitting on a stone at the entrance to a long avenue. The flagstones are warm beneath your bare feet and the air carries a faint hint of ambergris.

The avenue is guarded by ram-headed sphinxes which confront each other between high stone pillars. Upon the ground, the shadows are inky and the whole scene is one of silver and black. The silence is almost palpable. Overhead, myriads of stars blaze in the dark vault of heaven—another vista of silver and black.

You are dressed in a robe of fine, white linen which is held in place by a girdle of twisted cords. You realize that the avenue awaits, so you begin to walk steadily along it, the moonlight splashing cold between the pillars.

Eventually, you emerge into a vast courtyard, empty, and somehow alien. Ahead, broad steps lead up to a great doorway, flanked by two gleaming statues made entirely of gold. They are of the goddess, Maat, and represent truth and justice.

As you slowly and hesitantly climb the steps, the doors swing silently open, as if you are expected! It is then that you realize you are not alone! A jackal, black as jet, pads silently at your side. You sense it will not harm you. It does not even appear to notice you! It utters a low growl as the doors open, the long, pointed muzzle sniffing the interior. Then it darts forward and disappears inside. You follow, your heart pounding.

A faint light hovers in the gloom as you enter. It moves, as if beckoning, and your feet touch marble — smooth and cool — as you advance into the temple. Light from lamps, hanging from a high ceiling, reveal a huge pillared hall. The sweet odor of incense is stronger here. The walls are painted with pictures of the Egyptian gods and goddesses and moonbeams melt through the high windows.

Now, you perceive that a slim figure is carrying the hovering light. The captured flame gleams steadily through translucent alabaster. Your guide is naked. Reed-slim, oiled limbs reflect the flame, the bare buttocks undulating as the muscles move under the bronze skin. A long black wig caresses the slim back, tight curls bobbing from side to side. You follow meekly.

At the far end of the hall, your guide passes through an arched doorway covered by a reed curtain. It opens onto a narrow passage which penetrates deeper into the temple. Here, the walls are covered with hieroglyphics, which leap into life as the light catches them. Another curtain is lifted; a small hand holding it while you pass through, then you are alone.

Without the friendly lamp, the blackness is oppressive and you know not what to do. But presently, a pool of light shows in the distance, and a tall figure advances, silhouetted against the sudden brightness. You have entered a large circular room, where a round table stands centrally.

The figure is that of a young woman. She moves to the table and lights a lamp which is placed upon it. The face that turns to look at you reveals great calmness and serenity. She inclines her head and smiles, and you walk across to her.

The floor of this room is made from multi-colored, mosaic tiles, inlaid with precious stones. The pattern is of a great zodiac which gives way to other pictures and symbols, making it a mandala of universal knowledge.

"Sit down and rest." The voice has the clarity of a golden bell. Your companion indicates a chair and seats herself facing you.

The table is of obsidian, shining and dark, like a great lake, and your images are clearly reflected in its surface. A beaker of wine is offered, and you drink, thankfully. All the while, you are regarded steadily by a pair of wide, gray eyes which seem to understand all your hopes and fears. You gaze back and contemplate the face before you. The eyes and brows are blackened with kohl and the lips are stained crimson. The head-dress is composed of a single, upright feather, set at the side of the head and surmounting the customary Egyptian wig of gleaming black hair. The tiny ringlets fall to touch the well-formed breasts, over which a jewelled pectoral rests. Broad bracelets decorate the tops of the slim, brown arms, which are folded and resting on the table.

"My name is Maat, and I am the Goddess of Truth and Justice. My symbol is the Scales and you have been brought to this temple to view your position in the scheme of things." Maat smiles.

> "Be not dismayed; what is required of you is no more than can be comfortably endured. You will be given the unique opportunity of renewing the most important of your previous lives on Earth—the ones which contain the best and the worst of actions and indicate the extent of

soul development. The very fact that you are here at this moment in time reveals that your higher self is now taking charge. That is good!

"Over the centuries, the seed that is your soul has traversed many lives. I welcome you here as a starseed of the future. Starseeds are those souls who grow to become the Shining Ones, dwelling on the Plane of Masterhood. They have outgrown earthly bodies and take on flesh, solely for the benefit of humanity. The world knows them as Teachers. But, all stem from the one supreme source of life whose name is mystery of mysteries.

"Now that you have rested, it is time to confront your past. From this knowledge, you will gain enlightenment and understanding concerning your present life on Earth. Go and stand on the sign in which the Sun was placed at your birth."

Bare feet covering the shining patterns, you find your sign easily. The circular walls of this room are covered with bronze mirrors. The one which encompasses the degrees of your sign begins to glow, as if your coming has brought it to life. The red-gold metal pulsates, emitting a curious, humming tone which fills the room. Now, the throbbing rhythm seems to be inside your head accompanying your heartbeat! A chair is thrust beneath you and you drop into it—your eyes fixed upon the glowing mirror.

Suddenly, the mirror darkens again, and the vibrations are drawn back into its depths. In the same instant, you know instinctively that something has gone from you and has been absorbed into the speculum.

As you watch, a gray mist creeps over the surface. It swirls and shifts, becoming ever more dense, until the center clears and the vapor rolls back, as if pulled by a magical force.

And now, the speculum is filled with all manner of glowing pictures. What is shown to you may make you laugh or cry, feel angry, sorrowful or glad. The visions will evoke responses from your emotional body of feeling, and at the same time, inform your intellect. The experience is entirely personal.

You may recognize another soul with whom you have a karmic link, for whatever reason. If you have already met him or her again in this life, it will be your decision as to whether you deem it wise to inform to them about the part they play in your karmic record. If you feel they will understand—well and good.

You may even be shown your next life on Earth, although this is not a common occurrence. You will be informed only to the point of your own endurance and/or comprehension. If you see nothing, do not despair. This merely indicates that you are not quite ready for this kind of revelation. And you must try again in twelve months' time.

At last, the scenes fade, and the mirror resumes its original appearance. Maat comes to you, offering another beaker of wine. "Drink, then rest a while. The guide will lead you out. We shall meet again." She waits until you have drained the liquid, then leaves the room.

When you walk over to the curtain, the guide appears and leads you along the passage and through the great hall. As you step outside, the slinky form of the jackal glides to your side and accompanies you until you reach the Avenue of Sphinxes. Then, he, too, is gone.

Once more, you pass the great stone figures. The Moon has set and the horizon lightened to a faint, pinkish glow. The wine is taking its effect, so you sit at the base of a column, watching the sky.

Quite suddenly, the God of the Ancient Egyptians lifts over the horizon at the end of the avenue—huge and red. The white sphinxes leap into startled color—a flaming orange-red, their shadows slow-moving and deepest blue-black. As the scene fades, you hear, faintly, birds from their nests atop the columns, whistling and piping to the newborn day.

In your chair before the altar, sit still and digest the journey—the path of Libra. It is best to record your experiences as soon as possible, while they are still fresh in your mind. Though a view of previous lives can usually be recalled at will. Certainly, they will be helpful when studying the natal chart of your present life.

SCORPIO

OCTOBER 23RD–NOVEMBER 21ST

Planet: Pluto
Jewel: Topaz
Number: 9
Governs: Generative
       organs

Color: Magenta
Metal: Iron
Flower: Heather
Herb: Basil

Positive Traits
Powerful feelings and emotions; a sense of purpose;
discerning; subtle; determined; passionate; loyal.

Negative Traits
Jealous; secretive; suspicious; unreasonable; perverse.

SCORPIO

The Eighth House sign of death and loss,
with failing flame of yester's bright;
As nature sheds her weary dross,
escaping to immortal light.
The waters of the Styx flow by,
as Charon's boat awaits each call;
Yet weep not opal tears, nor sigh,
for all who live must surely fall.
The door's ajar to light the way,
for joyous spirits soaring high;
Farewell to shells of worn out clay,
for freedom gained is not to die.
The judgement of the meek or wild;
It matters most they did their best,
as gentle Ge reclaims each child
and Chitragupa marks its test.
In fearful depths of Hades realm,
where bones lie cold in Pluto's bed,
a lustful Mars now takes the helm,
to stir the flame and raise the dead.
The cycle joins at Hallowe'en,
as ageless myst'ries work their rite.
All time is NOW, for souls unseen —
the quick, the dead, as one, unite.

LEON G. DICKENS

SCORPIO

Scorpio is the second water sign and the third fixed sign of the zodiac. It is associated with death and regeneration and is one of the most complex of signs. The Scorpion portrays life and death very forcibly, living successfully in the arid desert with the death-dealing sting in its tail.

The combination of sexual and spiritual aspects are depicted by two other symbols, the serpent and the eagle. The serpent symbolizes sexual motivation and the chthonic powers in the depths of the earth, while the eagle reflects the wonderful transformation towards things of the spirit.

The discovery of Pluto in 1930 brought this planet to the position of Scorpio's ruler. The Mars factor partially expressed the sign, being the planet of desire, but Pluto, standing for the deep, unfathomable parts of the subconscious and as Lord of the Underworld, must surely be the sign's true ruler.

Though planets lie undiscovered, their influence can still affect our lives. When one is "found," however, it would appear in evolutionary terms to be the correct time for its influence to be recognized and become active on a worldwide scale.

After the discovery of Pluto, all kinds of obscure mental illnesses began to be seriously studied. Psychiatry and psychological phenomena were approached in a manner totally unknown previously.

As far as we know, Pluto is the planet furthest from the Sun and could be described as our galaxy's sentinel to the mysteries of the universe—like the sign of Scorpio, itself! When a planet is discovered, it seems to act as a herald—a numinous finger that points the way forward to new and unexplored territory.

The art of keeping secrets comes naturally to the soul in Scorpio. This sign speaks of fixed, or still, water which shows a calm, unruffled exterior. But what cauldron of emotions seethe beneath the smooth surface?

In a young soul, there are often scheming or revengeful thoughts all waiting to hatch out, and because of the outward calm, opponents are taken completely by surprise.

It is essential that the Scorpionic soul understands its great potential for emotion and directs it into positive channels. This, of course, comes with experience and time. It can be said that this sign is capable of the most intense and impassioned depth of feeling, "deeper than did ever plummet sound."

The love nature expresses a profound fidelity and mirrors the Biblical truth: "Love is strong as death. Many waters cannot quench love, neither can the floods drown it."

Beyond everything, Scorpio has endurance and tremendous powers of concentration. It will persist and follow its course, long after other souls have dropped by the wayside. Courage is one of the attributes, and often, genius is present here—directed towards the benefit of humanity.

The immense power of still water reflects the activity in the world around it. The soul digests and considers everything, but, in the end, it will formulate its own particular ideas and concepts.

A force to be reckoned with, the soul realizes that silence preserves and gives life to all kinds of magical thought. The intuition is very sharp and the intellectual faculties singularly piercing.

Solving the mystery of life is one of the preoccupations of this sign. There is much interest in that which is hidden or unknown. The work "occult" is a fascinating neon sign to these people. They yearn to penetrate the veil of the unseen, and often delve into the darker aspects of magic.

But, in the evolved soul there will be a deep, unsatisfied longing to be as the eagle, and soar beyond the confines of the material world. This naturally leads them to take initiation in a school of the mysteries. The Scorpion will take all the time necessary, in order to ensure that such a tradition is a genuine one, before considering the initial plunge into what may well prove to be a lifetime's commitment and study.

Once this sign gives its allegiance to a cause, woe betide anyone who dares to question the veracity of that cause. After all, if it is worthy of this sign's loyalty, it must indeed be all that is honorable and good!

The soul in Scorpio, has more than its fair share of troubles, but the attributes of determination and courage will see it through and often as the victor!

Because of an inborn depth of feeling, Scorpio can suffer to a great degree — and it does so in silence. Conversely, attainments and successes can prove to be the envy of others. Through the experiences of personal loss, the soul learns to look behind the mask of matter. When this occurs, it is no longer bound to the idea of separateness in creation and death. This illusion, once viewed as a concrete reality, fades as awareness of the life force — permeating all worlds, incorruptible and eternal — takes its place.

With this knowledge, the soul gains poise and a profound inner peace. It is also very close to discovering the mystery of Scorpio — the wisdom of the Gods. This sign is called, the "Well of the Water of Life." *Scorpio symbolizes regeneration of spirit and matter.*

Legends

Greek

Orion, a Greek giant, was said to have been conceived from the urine of three gods, namely, Zeus, Poseidon and Hermes. These three were traveling across Boeotia, when they encountered Hyrieus, a peasant, who, being ignorant of their identities, offered the gods hospitality at his humble cottage.

Eventually he was informed who his guests were, and immediately sacrificed an ox in their honor. Gratified by this token of fealty, the gods promised to grant Hyrieus a boon. The peasant then explained that his wife had died childless, and had made him promise he would not marry again. However, he told them he would much love a son—without a second marriage.

The gods consulted between themselves, then told Hyrieus to bring to them the hide of the ox. The peasant laid it before them, whereupon the gods urinated into it and told Hyrieus to bury it in the ground for nine months.

The command was obeyed, and when the skin was finally dug up it was found to contain a beautiful child. The peasant named the baby Urion (*ab urina*), a name which was later changed to Orion. He grew to gigantic stature and became famous for his exploits. The goddess, Artemis, heard of his fame and took him as one of her attendants. They would often hunt together— Orion's beauty being much admired by this virgin goddess.

One day, the giant boasted that he would kill every animal upon the Earth. When she heard this, the Earth sent to Orion a huge scorpion, which slew him with its sting. Thus, the Earth saved the animals, and the gods placed Orion in the heavens.

The constellation of Orion the Hunter rises in the east, the moment that the constellation of the Scorpion sinks from view in the west. So the two groups of stars are never seen above the horizon at the same time. Considering the legend, this is not surprising!

Egyptian

Selket (Selquet), the Scorpion goddess of the Egyptian pantheon, was one of the four goddesses who guarded the sarcophagus of the young Tut-ankh-Amon. She stands with winged arms extended in a gesture of protection and wears the *khaet* headdress surmounted by a scorpion. As the fourth of the tutelary deities, she protected the intestines of the Pharaoh and shared this task with the hawk-headed Qebhsnuf.

As the Scorpion goddess, Selket was closely associated with the genitals, and was often invoked as the guardian of conjugal bliss. At the temple of Deir el Bahri, she joins Neith in a hieroglyph of the heavens. The two goddesses are seen protecting Amon and the queen-mother from any interference.

In some of the ancient texts, Selket was regarded as a daughter of Ra, the Sun-god, and was depicted as an actual scorpion with a woman's head.

Plutarch speaks of the god, Set, sending a scorpion to kill the child Horus, the son of Isis and Osiris. Horus did indeed die of the bite, but Ra magically revived him.

Sumerian/Babylonian

The famous exploits of Gilgamesh, the great hero of Sumer and Babylon, are immortalized in an epic poem of great length. This masterpiece of Babylonian literature was found written upon a series of clay tablets in the palace library of Ashurbanipal, a king of Assyria.

The twelve cantos each contain some three hundred verses relating to the adventures of this giant figure, who, some say, was a king of Erech. Certainly, his exploits rival those of the Greek, Hercules. The ninth tablet states, "two thirds of him is god, one third is man." Even so, Gilgamesh went in search of the secret of immortality.

In one adventure, the hero attempted to pass through the gate of sunrise, set between twin mountain peaks. He encountered the scorpion-man who guarded the gate and decided to consult Uta-Nap-ishtim, a man who had survived the great floods and upon whom the gods had bestowed immortality.

The perils of that journey were considerable, yet Gilgamesh would face them: "If I meet lions and am afraid, I shall raise my head and call upon Sin; To Ishtar, courtesan of the gods, my prayers shall rise."

He reached a twin-peaked mountain, where, every night, the sun sank and rested. The huge gates of this mountain were protected by scorpion-men whose great heads reached the domain of the gods and whose feet touched the center of the earth. Their dazzling brilliance overthrew mountains and Gilgamesh was struck with horror at the sight, but his courage gradually returned and he knelt humbly before them.

One of the scorpion-men perceived that the hero was more god than man and forthwith offered to show Gilgamesh the way through the mountains. After eleven double hours of striding through darkness, he emerged and found himself in a beautiful garden which lay near the sea. The tree of the gods stood in this place. Its branches were made of lapis lazuli and all manner of precious stones were strewn beneath it.

Miscellaneous

A 12th century manuscript, the *Ancren Riwle,* is one of religious instruction. It describes the scorpion as "a kind of serpent that has a face like that of a woman and puts on a pleasant countenance." This is another example of how the female was denigrated and always linked with the Christian concept of evil, *i.e.,* the scorpion or serpent!

Rosalynde (1590) a work by one Thomas Lodge, contains this passage: "They that are stung by the scorpion cannot be recovered but by the scorpion." Considering the later scientific experiments of Edward Jenner, this statement is interesting, for Jenner discovered that immunity from disease could be attained by giving the patient small doses of the same toxin, a remedy which became known as vaccination!

The Rite of Scorpio

When the Sun has entered the sign of Scorpio, it is time to prepare your altar. Light the candle and sit down in your chair. This rite starts with a period of contemplation upon transformation.

Bring the mind to consider the manifest and its many forms, and realize that this world, and everything connected with it, is subject to change. Plants, animals, human beings, stars and planets, all have a beginning and an apparent ending.

Change occurs because the forces of the unmanifest, which bring everything into being, are constantly creating new life forms. Therefore, the world of form, as we perceive it, is the unreal, however solid it may appear, and the unseen energies of the unmanifest are the real, and exist continually.

Matter or form is an illusion, and in the East it is called "Maya," meaning illusion. Matter is transitory and is in a constant process of renewal. It is the veil of the unmanifest through which the miracle of life is wrought.

All life forms have rhythms of life, death and rebirth, the only difference is in the *length* of the lifespan.

Our position in the scheme of things enables us to view both the partial life of a star, and the life of a microbe with equal facility. This is not to say that the extent of our vision encompasses the whole of existence. What is seen through telescope and microscope is but a fragment of something quite beyond our comprehension.

In the month of October and the Sun's passage through the sign of Scorpio, the energies of the vegetable kingdom are being withdrawn and returned to their source—the unmanifest world. This action is shown in the glyph of Scorpio, thus: ♏. Thoughts turn towards the mysteries of life and death, and to those who have shuffled off this mortal coil. It is a time when the veil between the worlds becomes very thin indeed. Hence, a time when communication with loved ones who have gone before is possible, or more easily accomplished, than at other times of the year.

The festival of Samhain, or Hallowe'en, which lies in the center of Scorpio, is the Celebration of the Dead, and reveals that our ancestors were fully aware of the implications concerning this time of the year. They lived their lives in harmony with the Nature Year and through their knowledge of the zodiac.

Gaze steadily above the flame of the candle, then close your eyes and begin your visualization.

♏ ♏ ♏ ♏

The stone slab you are leaning against is ice cold to your back. It is late evening and a mist hangs low over the ground. There is dampness everywhere and you recognize the faint smell of rotting vegetation. A light drizzle begins to fall and drops of moisture trickle from your hair and find their way down your neck, making you shiver. The dampness is seeping into your body, so you stand up, easing cramped limbs. As you do so, your feet strike a stone bar and you realize that this place is an old graveyard. You have been sitting upon a grave with the headstone at your back!

The mist hangs, like a gray pall, and somewhere, far off, an owl hoots, mournfully. The tombstones lean drunkenly, at awkward angles, and the box-like bulk of tombs, their capstones broken, gape like cavernous mouths. What a forsaken place!

The remains of a path threads its way through the graves and you follow it, the long grass tangling and pulling at your feet. A church bell chimes the hour, its tone, muffled and flat in the mist. Surely, this path leads somewhere?

Suddenly, your feet find a flagstone and you step onto a broad path where yew trees almost meet overhead. Here, the going is easier and you are able to make out the way ahead. Your clothing is now thoroughly wet and clinging coldly to your limbs. What would you give to be soaking in a hot bath!

A rustling turns your head and your heart thumps uncomfortably. But the gray curtain merely reveals the black fingers of crosses, pointing to the sky.

Your foot meets a clump of moss, growing between the stones, and you almost go down. Recovering, you peer ahead and discern a small glimmer of light in the distance. Hurrying now, the light hangs steadily and becomes brighter. Of course — the church! Every grave-yard has one!

The mist thins to reveal crumbling stone walls, and a door, where a lantern hangs. Your trembling fingers find a rusty iron ring. You turn it, and push. The door yields, reluctantly. Inside the pitch blackness is all enveloping, and you can only stand, mustering your courage. The smell of dank, fetid air assails your nostrils and you long to turn and run, *but you do not!*

As your eyes become accustomed to the interior, you can just see the high windows where a grayness hovers, as if it, too, hesitates to enter. Your mind springs to life again — of course, the lamp outside! Slipping through the door you take the lantern from its hook and holding it high, you re-enter the church.

The main body of the building lies to the right; the dusty pews queueing one behind the other. But now, you see another door, straight ahead, and this one is slightly ajar with broken steps leading down into more murky darkness. It takes all your courage not to drop the light and run — anywhere! Even the silent graves are preferable at this moment. But something holds you to your quest. Have you come *this* far to allow fear the upper hand?

Surprisingly, this door opens easily as if on newly oiled hinges, and gripping the lantern for dear life, you begin the descent. The stairway winds like a corkscrew, but the bottom is reached without mishap. The light reveals an arched passage, and glancing up, you encounter two glittering, green eyes watching your every movement from a recess in the wall.

Sudden fear gnaws in your belly as the snake, disturbed from sleep, hisses its annoyance, the forked tongue, darting, as if to smother the flame. Unable to move, you stare at the shining undulations, working and furling rhythmically. Then, swiftly, it moves down the wall and vanishes into the darkness. Your heart steadies, and carefully, you continue along the narrow way.

The passage opens into a large crypt. Stone pillars support the roof and run into arches above your head. A bat careers wildly past your outstretched arm, startled by the intrusion. What now? Timidly, you move through the columns and suddenly, your face is against a soft, velvety material. This curtain apparently cuts the crypt in half. Pulling feverishly at the cloth, you feel for an opening, and find one. Then you gasp and cry out with relief. There is light beyond the screen—much light! Tall-standing, wrought-iron candlesticks, each holding as many as nine candles, encircle a rough-hewn stone altar. The glowing light and gentle heat draw you inside this haven.

A brazier gleams red in a corner, and, from the hot coals, the sweet smoke of incense spirals upwards. The snake lies coiled upon the altar, the green and gold skin reflecting the candlelight. Within its coils stands a plain wooden cup and a platter of bread. The calming effect of this temple destroys any apprehension, and involuntarily, you kneel, allowing its ambience to wash over you.

How long you stay like that, you are not sure, but there is an unwillingness to let the moment slip away.

The sound of approaching footsteps brings you to your feet and you look around for a place of concealment. An alcove provides dark shadow and you shrink back against the stone wall.

The footsteps halt and you hear a door open and close. Whoever the visitor is, he or she is now in the temple and only a few feet from your hiding-place! Holding your breath, you peer cautiously round the edge of the wall. A cowled and robed figure stands before the altar, and, as if your presence is already discerned, it drops the cowl and turns in your direction.

"Fear not, I will not harm you." The tone is grave, yet holds a slight hint of amusement. The features are those of an elderly man, and he is smiling, kindly. His white hair hangs over the dark robe, but, surprisingly, his folded hands hold the suppleness of youth. Slowly, you emerge and stand, defiantly, a hand gripping the cool metal of a nearby candlestick.

"I did not know who or what to expect," you explain, lamely.

"I know, child, I know. It has been quite an arduous adventure, has it not?" He nods, understandingly. "Still, you have overcome the test. You have not faltered, and that is good."

You wonder about him. His straight, upright carriage belies his apparent age and he carries himself with great dignity.

"My name is not important, child, but all come to know me, sooner or later. May I offer you the Cup?" Like others you have met on these adventures, this person knows what you are thinking! He moves to the altar and lifts up the cup.

"Drink!" The well-formed fingers caress the vessel lovingly, and in a moment, you have taken it, your lips closing on the rim. You are not at all sure what kind of fluid you are drinking. One second it tastes like water, the next, like wine, and now—like milk!

"It is the Moon's liquid and entirely magical," again he answers your thoughts! You thank him and he replaces the cup.

"Will you also consume some bread?" He offers the platter and you suddenly realize how hungry you are!

The bread is extremely wholesome and you busily crunch three pieces.

"That was very good. Thank you."

He returns the platter to its position upon the altar and gently strokes the snake's smooth head.

"This altar is one of the oldest in the world. It, and others like it, are dedicated to the Magna Mater, the Great Mother. In Egypt and elsewhere, temples to the Gods were raised upon an underground sanctuary such as this. You will visit one of them in another journey."

He motions for you to sit down and you sink onto a small footstool.

"The Great Mother is the giver and the receiver. She gives life and She also takes life. They who believe in the Great Mother are Her especial Children. They, unlike those who know Her not, are guided in life and also in their rebirth.

"Most of mankind are orphaned of the Mother. The vital link has been severed. To believe that divinity is wholly male is an error, and, moreover, an insult to the source of life. By denying the feminine in religious thought, a blockage occurs on all levels—spiritual, emotional and physical. As a consequence of this bereavement, the individual often senses that something is wrong—something is missing, and he or she may attempt to correct this state of affairs by following beliefs other than their own. Always hoping to be healed, to be made whole.

"Again and again, they are disappointed, until they find the Great Mother in their travels. In recognizing the Goddess, nothing is lost, because She immediately reveals Her opposite— Her complementary counterpart—Her consort and lover, Pan, the virile God of Nature. From these two, come all other Gods; mostly watered down versions of the originals, and therefore pallid ghosts in comparison. Now, I will show you something."

He moves behind the altar and you follow, obediently. A small door is hidden in the shadows, and your companion opens it. Steps lead down to a broad river where a large, black barge is moored. The water is an inky blue-black and reflects a thin, waning moon.

"This is the river of the Moon, and all are taken to the other side. The ancient Greeks knew it as the Styx— the River of the Dead." He looks into your face. "But, fear not, death is not the end. Rather is it a new beginning."

"Who are you?" the question springs unbidden to your lips. He gazes into the distance. "I have many names. I was Thanatos to the aesthetic Greeks; Seker Osiris to the ancient Egyptians; the Dagda to the Celts, yet, I am also the transformer. Taking bodies and regenerating them—giving new life." He grins, disarmingly, and looks almost boyish, "Is that so very terrible?"

You grin back and shake your head. "No. I am glad that I have met you at this time. By what name may *I* call you?"

"How about Nicholas—will that do?"

You nod in agreement and he takes your hands between both of his and closes his eyes. A feeling of great power and strength surges through your entire body. It feels like being lit up from within—as though you had touched the Fount of Life, itself.

Then, Nicholas draws you back inside. "You must go back—now."

Strangely, there is reluctance on your part.

"I hope you will return from time to time and bring others with you. Perhaps upon the next solar return to Scorpio?" You agree, happily, and he leads you out of the temple, along the passage and up the winding steps to the door of the church. You wave Nicholas goodbye and walk slowly back through the graveyard. The fog has lifted, and a sheet of sunlight bathes the place in brightness.

Without any difficulty, you find the spot where you began this journey, and sit down. Your gaze is drawn to a clear sky where an eagle soars on powerful wings, silhouetted against the azure vault of heaven. It circles once, then is gone, and at last, the vision fades.

Take a little to eat and drink and give thanks before the altar. A candle must be left burning throughout the night, to symbolize the immortality of the soul and as a remembrance of Nicholas.

SAGITTARIUS

NOVEMBER 22ND – DECEMBER 21ST

Planet: Jupiter
Jewel: Turquoise
Number: 3
Governs: Thighs, Liver,
      Hepatic system

Color: Purple
Metal: Tin
Flower:
Chrysanthemum
Herb: Sage

Positive Traits

Jovial; optimistic; philosophical; frank; sincere; dependable.

Negative Traits

Careless; tactless; extreme; capricious; timid; old-fashioned.

SAGITTARIUS

SAGITTARIUS

O'er restless tides that ebb and flow,
an arch of promise, steadfast, true;
As Freedom's Centaur bends his bow,
His mark the winter—half-way through.
The battle rages, day and night,
yet Jupiter keeps a steady helm;
And guides the Gods of Dark and Light
from winter's cold, to warmer realm.
From deep within the sleeping soil,
where yesters loved ones lie at rest;
The workshop of the world doth toil,
on clay discarded, souls thrice blest.
Within Earth's Hall of Consecration,
Aladdin's Cave of gems and gold,
The Mystery of Regeneration—
Eternal Gift of "new for old."

LEON G. DICKENS

SAGITTARIUS

Sagittarius is the third fire sign and the third mutable sign of the zodiac. Its ruler is the greater benefic—Jupiter. Sagittarius is the third dispensation of the Godhead—that of the Spirit.

The symbol of this sign is the Archer with his arrow aiming at the star-studded universe. The Archer is none other than Chiron, the noble centaur of the ancient Greeks. With the body of a horse and the torso and head of a man, Chiron depicts the higher self in full control of the animal or desire nature. The archer symbolizes the swiftness and restlessness of the soul born in Sagittarius. Its brilliance and impermanence speeds through the environment like a meteor, which all too soon is gone, leaving friends sorrowing that this is so.

As opposed to the intense clear fire of Aries, and the ardent love-heat of Leo, the lambent flame of Sagittarius represents the fire of the soul, and this kind of fire is likened to that ambience portrayed around the heads of saints. It is the ephemeral beauty of the Aurora Borealis and the Aurora Australis, the northern and southern lights and of the mysterious luminance known as will-o-the-wisp and jack-o-lantern, which move eerily over fens and marshes, usually in the fog or at dead of night. It is also likened to that which is called St. Elmo's fire, a phosphorescent light that plays round the yards and masts of sea-going vessels at the height of a storm.

As befits mutable fire, it permeates all levels of existence and appears in a variety of guises. It invigorates the tallest trees and the smallest animals. In 1858, the work of an industrial chemist, Baron Karl von Reichenbach, revealed that radiation comes from plants, crystals, animals and humans and can be detected and seen under certain conditions. It was called Odic Force.

Under the beneficence of Jupiter, Sagittarius speaks of the beauty of nature and teaches us that respect for all life on this planet must be nurtured in the heart of all people. On a subliminal level, the flame of Sagittarius is the flame of inspiration and is that sudden illumination spoken of by poets and artists.

In this mutable sign, the soul lives through the extremes of exaltation and despondency. Religion is very important and many diverse faiths and beliefs will be tried and often found wanting. The soul's view of the spiritual is far beyond that of humanity in general. And yet, the soul can be hidebound and old-fashioned in a moral sense, and in matters of religion, it often prefers the orthodox. This is the paradox of the sign, and often depends on the soul's evolutionary status.

The love of freedom is important, though the soul is innately timid. It is not averse to liaisons or affairs, but if these conflict with the status-quo they will be kept secret.

At first, the young soul, like a frightened horse, shies away from anything connected with responsibility. Contact with the higher mind will often come from a divine discontent and the realization that travel and the new experience does not entirely satisfy.

At last, the eloquent child finds the arrow of light illuminating the man or woman within. And then, under the fortunate rays of Jupiter, the lawgiver of the stars, the enlightened soul becomes a source of wisdom and inspiration to all, often holding a high office.

All the verdant growth and luxuriance of nature, including the majestic beauty of the great trees, comes under the providence of Jupiter. With such an *embarras*

de richesses there is no wonder that the soul is intoxicated with life and has an inner certainty that it was
born with more than its fair share of luck.

Quite obviously, Sagittarius is an oasis in the
zodiac. After the soul-purging, yet entirely necessary
sojourn in Scorpio, the soul is given the rainbow of
cheerfulness and hope; a chance to experience the light-
hearted and optimistic side of living. And why not?

This third and final fire sign fuses the meanings of
Aries and Leo. The great spur of Sagittarius is one of
aspiration and quite literally, the starry sky is the only
limit. With speed and grace the arrow is aimed, then
loosed upon infinity in the quest for truth. This sign is
called the "traveller to the stars." *Sagittarius symbolizes joi
de vivre!*

Legends

Greek
Although the name of the archer is found in the earlier
Babylonian astrology, in recent times Sagittarius is usually identified with the Greek legend of Chiron, the
centaur.

He was born from a union between Cronus, father
of Zeus, the Philyra, daughter of Oceanus. Like numerous other unions of the gods, the encounter was not
desired by the woman, and was virtually a rape. One
source states that in order to escape, Philyra turned
herself into a mare, whereupon Cronus covered her as a
stallion. Another suggests that the couple were surprised in the act by Rhea, wife to Cronus – so, in order
to save face, the god took the form of a stallion and
galloped away!

Whatever the truth of the matter, in due course,
Philyra was delivered of a child who was half-man, half-

horse. The poor woman could not bear to look upon or even think about this monster to which she had given birth. She prayed to be changed into some other form of life and her prayers were quickly answered. Zeus took pity on her plight and transformed her into a linden tree.

In spite of all the uproar at his birth, Chiron grew up quite happily in a cave on Mount Pelion, and in time, he married the nymph, Chariclo, a friend of Athene. He was educated by Artemis and Apollo and became renowned in the arts of hunting, pipe-playing, soothsaying, healing and medicine. His fame as a doctor, prophet and scholar spread rapidly and he was known as Son of Philyra and King of the Centaurs.

Chiron reared and educated many children of the famous including Diomedes (or Jason), Asclepius, Aeneas, Medeius, and his own grandson, Achilles. They, in their turn, grew up to become heroes in one way or another.

Chiron had a daughter who became the prophetess, Thetis. Zeus chose Peleus, son of Endeis, to be her husband, but Chiron knew that Thetis, being immortal like himself, would not agree to the union. Therefore, he gave Peleus certain instructions to overcome any obstinacy on his daughter's part.

At King Chiron's cave, Peleus hid behind a myrtle bush, and when Thetis came to the cave for her midday sleep, Peleus awakened her with a kiss. Instantly, Thetis changed successively into a burning fire, running water, a great lion and a serpent. But, Peleus, having been warned of this by Chiron, held on to her firmly. Finally, when Thetis realized the stubbornness of her admirer, she turned herself into a huge, slippery cuttlefish and covered him with sticky blue-black ink. But through all this torment, Peleus hung on to her for dear life and at last, Thetis yielded and melted into his embrace.

Hera summoned all the Olympians, and the wedding was celebrated at Chiron's now famous home on Mount Pelion. The gods were seated on twelve thrones. Zeus gave the bride away and Hera presented the bridal torch. Ganymede, the cup-bearer to Zeus, poured nectar into silver goblets, while the Muses and the Fates filled the air with melodious songs. A spiral dance was performed by fifty Nereids, while hundreds of centaurs, wearing chaplets made from grass and holding darts of fir, predicted good fortune for the couple. From this union was born Achilles.

Although Chiron was an immortal, the time came when he grew weary of his long life. His friend, Hercules, unknowingly, was to play a part in this. Hercules had been busy putting down a group of wayward centaurs when the last parting arrow struck Chiron on the knee, although he had not been involved in the fight. Screaming with pain, Chiron hobbled to his refuge where Hercules drew out the barb and applied healing unguents to the centaur's instructions. But the pain persisted and became another reason why Chiron wished to depart this life.

Hercules grieved for his friend and resolved to try and help him. He remembered a promise made to him by his father, Zeus. This concerned one Prometheus, a mortal, who had been punished by Zeus for giving the gift of fire to his own kind. He was fastened to a rock for eternity, and if this were not enough, an eagle came each night to gorge on his liver!

Largely as a result of the entreaties of Hercules, Zeus had agreed that if an immortal would relinquish his immortality, Prometheus would go free. Accordingly, Hercules attended Zeus and explained the situation. Chiron eagerly gave up his immortality and Zeus placed him in the heavens where he became a part of the constellation of Sagittarius.

Chinese
Ch'ang-o or Heng-o, the beautiful Goddess of the Moon, was married to an illustrious personage known as I, the Excellent Archer.

In Chinese legend, it is said that when the Earth was young, there were ten suns in the sky; one for each hour of the day. But, one morning, all ten suns rose at the same time and the Earth was in grave danger of being shriveled up. I, the Excellent Archer, saved the situation by drawing his magic bow and shooting down nine of the suns, and as a reward for his bravery, the gods gave I the drug of immortality.

His wife, however, swallowed the drug, herself, and in order to escape from the wrath of her husband, she fled to the Moon and made it her home. I, the Excellent Archer, pursued his wife, but the hare who lives in the moon fought with I and persuaded him to abandon his ideas of punishment. Ever after, I paid regular visits to see Ch'ang-o, and peace was restored.

The Rite of Sagittarius

When the Sun illuminates the sign of Sagittarius, prepare the altar and light a purple candle. Begin with a period of contemplation along the following lines.

The subtle message of Sagittarius informs us that humans must show respect for their brethren of the animal kingdom, since one is dependent upon the other. Up to now, humans have abused the animals, adhering to the Biblical assertion that they were put upon the Earth for our benefit! This statement is, of course, morally wrong. Homo sapiens may be a little higher on the Tree of Life, but the animals can still teach us much in the way of behavior patterns.

Many people believe that the flesh and blood of animals is good for them, and they continue to slaughter immense numbers in the most inhuman fashion. The enjoy the taste of meat—and unlike vegetarians, carnivores do not bother to investigate other sources of protein. In modern society, many do not have any concern for animal welfare. The horrors of factory farms and other similar establishments are allowed to continue. Most people do not even know how the joint of lamb or side of beef comes to be upon their table.

And we must not forget the approach of certain religions, where an animal has to be bled and, as a result, dies very slowly. Then, there are animals in the wild, which men hunt and kill for financial gain, often to the point of extinction of certain species.

Those who care for animals, and who have any kind of magical ability, must work in their own way to achieve some improvement in regard to the overall treatment of animals. The power of the great God Pan must be invoked in order to gain a new status for our brethren of the wildwood and of the factory farm.

Now, prepare for the visualization. Clear your mind of all extraneous thoughts. Gaze at the aura of your candle flame, then close your eyes.

⟋ ⟋ ⟋ ⟋

Your astral eyes open upon the steamy, lush vegetation of the jungle. The heavy, sweet perfume of strange flowers pervades the air while their vivid colors relieve the green tones of growth. The tops of the trees are lit with light from a westering sun; the near horizontal rays penetrating the thick foliage in thin, laser-like streaks.

For the moment, you are content to lie there, experiencing the wildness of the place, until a movement in the undergrowth catches your attention. The leaves part to reveal the face of a magnificent tiger! You merely watch, with great interest, as the beast emerges and sniffs the air in your direction.

It yawns widely, displaying dagger-sharp teeth and a long pink tongue. Slowly, it glides into the clearing to lie down a little way from your resting-place, the exotic stripes gleaming in the last rays of the sun. The huge, amber eyes look at you benignly, and suddenly, you feel a longing to express your gladness and appreciation of all animals.

It is said that long ago, when the world was young, there existed a time when it was possible to communicate with the animal kingdom. But the bond of trust was broken when we usurped the privilege and began killing wild life.

Your mind hovers over the tiger and you attempt to transmit feelings of affection and understanding towards it. How many tears would it take to wash away all the crimes of humanity? How can one small individual communicate the sorrow felt for all the cruelty and bloodshed? You cover your face, unable to come to terms with the emotions welling up from within. This world is truly hell for many creatures.

Something rough and moist touches your flesh, and behold, the tiger has come to you and is licking your hand! A sound, as of a great engine, begins in the animal's throat. It is purring—it senses your remorse and your humanity. It pushes its head against your side and you gently stroke the velvety coat.

At last, it moves away and settles down again on the grass. You look at one another in mutual understanding, then the amber eyes seem to grow larger and you feel that something unusual is about to occur. You are not sure what, but now you sense things from the *animal's* viewpoint, and everything is suddenly seen from a different perspective. It is as though you are actually *seeing* through the *eyes* of the tiger! The movement of leaves becomes sharper; colors appear less bright; things at a distance are seen more clearly than those close at hand.

The sun sinks even lower, and the tiger stands up, stretches itself, and disappears into the jungle. *And still you are looking through its enigmatic eyes!* In this way, the life of the animal is open to you. Another experience!

The scent of many things assails its nostrils and it is aware of other unseen inhabitants of the jungle simply through its olfactory organ! Their spoors are everywhere, crisscrossing over the ground. An antelope has recently passed this way; a panther is hidden in a tree above, and the familiar odor of the tiger's mate creates a bond, even at a distance—where she guards her young. The tiger feels a sudden urge to return to her, but the gnawing pangs of hunger are stronger, and must be satisfied.

The animal moves rapidly and soon the edge of the jungle is reached. The tiger pads along over an area of scrub, strewn with boulders, and the smell of water begins. A few more strides and the lake is in view, shining and clear and painted red by the sunset.

The tiger crouches now, belly to the ground, surveying the scene and the various forms of wildlife taking an evening drink.

A family of water buffalo snuffle their way along the bank, and hippos stand in the shallows looking like gray, oil-smooth boulders. All manner of birdlife is here, floating or flying over the water. Herons stand, stiff-legged, skewering fish with lance-sharp bills.

Flamingoes—a pink and white carpet of color, wade on scarlet legs or stand like sentinels, one leg hooked up under snowy wings. The tiger watches and waits.

A small group of ibex approach to slake their thirst. Restless and nervous, their heads dart up jerkily, nostrils quivering, as they measure the wind. But the tiger knows he is *downwind* of them.

One moves away from the rest, picking its way daintily among the rushes. The tiger flattens, ears back, perfectly concealed. He starts to inch forward, brushing the bleached tufts of coarse grass, and still the life around the lake is unaware of his presence.

The last cover, a jagged rock, is reached—a short run from the quarry. Then, in an instant, the tiger leaps forward. Too late, the young ibex races for the shelter of the herd. With a bound, the tiger is upon it, the water scattering in a thousand droplets around the pair. The kill is swift as the great jaws meet in the soft neck; hot blood staining the surface of the lake. The carcass is dragged onto dry land and the tiger appeases his hunger.

All but the hippos have fled; the sound of the stampede receding into the silence. The startled cries of birds abate, and the lake settles into its usual tranquillity.

All this you have experienced from the tiger's viewpoint. Like many other species, the tiger kills in order to live. Like most humans, it is a carnivore, but that is where the similarity ends. Unlike human beings, the tiger does not expect another animal to do its killing for it. It has the courage to perform the act, itself!

Half the carcass is saved, and after a drink, the tiger carries it back to feed the rest of his family. As it gazes over the water, replete, your link with the animal dissolves, and you realize that you are in the middle of a jungle, with night fast approaching.

You stand up, stretching stiff limbs, then, for want of a better direction, you head off along a somewhat indistinct track. The going is difficult, as the path all but disappears beneath a welter of trailing vegetation which catches at your feet, as if trying to prevent your progress.

The noises of the jungle at night begin. Weird cries and calls, which make the heart miss a beat, are all around. There seems no end to the tortuous meanderings of the track—which has disintegrated into a soggy morass of rotting undergrowth—a place where the sun never shines.

You take another weary step—and the ground vanishes! You plunge down into nothingness! Your scream of fright hits stone walls and multiplies alarmingly in your ears. The fall is broken by a large rope net, hanging in the darkness. The breath is knocked out of you and it is some time before you realize what has happened. You lie, spreadeagled, like a fly caught in a gigantic spider's web.

"How to escape from the Web of Fate—*that* is the problem!" The voice suddenly booms in the vacuum of the pit. Was it *really* a voice or merely the imaginings of your distraught mind? But, already, the net is being lowered, as if the giant hand had seized it. Down, down into the pitch blackness, you descend—coming to rest upon cold stone. Scrambling to your feet, you cannot see a thing, but something, or someone, has a hand in this adventure, so you wait.

A grating noise, as of a door opening, comes from the stygian darkness. And in that darkness is a gleam of light, swaying, as if carried in a hand. You wait. You do not call out.

Now, the clip-clopping of hooves attends the glow, and presently, a figure, tall and bearded, appears beside

the lantern he carries. A friendly, concerned countenance looks down on you, but you gasp in astonish-
ment, as the bare, bronzed torso gives way to the body
of a chestnut stallion! The broad flanks gleam in the
yellow light.

"I am Chiron, the centaur, and I welcome you to my
sign of the zodiac!" He places the lantern on a ledge and
retrieves a stone bottle which he offers to you.

"Here, drink some wine while I explain things."

The wine is dark and bittersweet. Very soon it
glows inside you and its warmth puts new life into your
limbs. Chiron folds his arms, and speaks:

"Now, the Web of Fate is the zodiac and the
placing of the stars at birth. It depends on the
condition of the karma you have inherited as to
whether it binds you, or not. An understanding
of the star pattern, or natal chart, is a necessity
for all who would attempt initiation.

"After studying the pattern, look carefully at the
12th house. If this is free from negative aspects,
well and good. You can be sure a heavy karmic
debt will not ensue.

"Then, see where my planet, great Jupiter, is
positioned, for *there* lies your Crock of Gold in
this life. The house he inhabits will reveal the
type of fortune he brings. It will come to you of
its own accord. I will go now, and wait for you
outside. I will leave you the light, and a problem to solve. The problem is to think of a way
this net might be raised to its original hanging
position, as it was before it was lowered to
release you."

Chiron departs, and the sound of hoofbeats fades into the distance. You turn and examine the skeins of thick rope trailing at your feet. There is no controlling apparatus—no pulley with which to raise it. You smile, ruefully, *that* would be too easy! The answer must lie in the metaphysical realms! You puzzle over the enigma, and then remember that Chiron called it the Web of Fate, and that this was another name for the zodiac!

You begin to concentrate upon the zodiac—the great circle—the Girdle of Venus. But, it is difficult to hold it in your mind for long. You bring your will to bear on the matter and double your efforts. With great determination, you mentally build each sign, in order of sequence, and try to visualize the rope as a scattering of stars with the signs turning on its edges.

After holding this picture in your mind for some time, the rope, amazingly, gives a few half-hearted flaps, rises, then plummets once more to the ground.

You try again, and the same thing happens. What are you doing wrong? You are obviously on the right track, but there is something missing from the mental picture you are forming.

You sit down and think on the problem. What did Chiron say? You ponder on his words and realize the value of *listening*—of giving your whole attention to what is being said to you. Often, the most interesting information is lost through lack of concentration.

You recall that the centaur mentioned your natal chart. Is that the key? Slowly, you attempt to build a mental image of the chart. This is more difficult because there is so much detail it is almost impossible to hold the entire pattern in your mind. You bring your will to bear again and make another effort . . . and at last, the web starts to rise. Then a wonderful thing occurs. As the rope ascends, it gradually changes into a sparkling, silvery material—a huge, gossamer network.

Tiny stars in jewelled colors appear, as though caught in the delicate strands. Then, the entire structure shivers and is transformed into the pattern of your own celestial configuration. The wonder of it holds you in thrall, and you begin to study it. Where your attention faltered, a sign or a planet pulsates intermittently. But still, on the whole, you are pleased with your efforts.

As the stars hang above you, two things happen. Your neck begins to ache from its awkward angle, and the darkness of the pit lifts, and is bathed in a soft, glowing light.

You laugh in sheer exuberance, and the stars tremble and emit a sweet, mellifluous, tinkling sound, as if they are rejoicing with you. The light grows stronger to become a shade of palest amethyst. The star pattern begins to dissolve—it is time to leave.

Picking up the lantern, you pass through the doorway in the rock and walk along a passage. What you have experienced in the pit still commands your attention. It has been brought very forcibly to bear upon you that there is a strong link between the stars and mankind. *That* which moves the stars, must also control our destiny, as was taught of old.

There was a supreme element of love and gentleness in the vision which left you breathless with joy— and a carefree sense of thinking that most of our troubles are of our own making—as indeed, they are! You are aware that this knowledge lies dormant, buried deep within the subconscious mind.

The passage starts to slope upwards and an opening can be seen ahead. An effulgence of amethyst-colored light fills the entrance as you emerge. You are standing upon a wide plateau with high cliffs at your back. The air is clean and fresh and you breath it with relief.

Mountain peaks are all around but fade into relative insignificance, as you stare, in disbelief, at the tallest of them. It is the most beautiful, being formed from pure amethyst crystals ranging in color from pale hues, to the deep purple brilliance of that stone. The entire scene is bathed in color from the mountain which glows and sends forth incandescent rays of light, as though it is mysteriously lit from within.

As you look upon it, you seem to see faces and dim figures in the crystal depths peeping out at you from time to time. These beings are fair to behold and remind you of the fairy legends of your childhood.

And now, Chiron appears, stroking his great beard. "I see you have solved the problem I gave you." He chuckles, and seems well-pleased with your efforts.

"Approach all future ones with the same clarity of vision and you will not go far wrong. Yonder, is the Mountain of Amethyst. It links with the higher octaves of Sagittarius and is a sign of wisdom gained.

"The stone has many virtues. It bestows tranquillity and induces mental clarity and prevision. What is more, it protects the traveler and is a bringer of light at any level.

"The beings you see within it are the elementals of the Earth Plane, who are under the protection of their benefactor, great Jupiter."

Chiron produces a small crystal of amethyst.
"Hold this in your hands for a moment and make a wish—a sensible one, mind." The centaur grins, "Now, throw it up as high as you can."

With a will, you hurl the jewel into the air, then gasp, as it soars ever higher! Chiron fixes an arrow to his bow and aims carefully. The dart leaps from the bowstring and wings after its quarry. The impact occurs in a blaze of light—a meteor shower of shining stars which fall slowly into the valley far below.

The centaur puts an arm around your shoulders and laughs at your expression of wonder.

"It is good for the soul to be occasionally astonished, or jogged out of its complacency." He winks, conspiratorially. "Now . . . watch!"

The sound, as of a great waterfall, fills the air, and far off, huge columns of froth and spume gush from a cleft in one of the mountain peaks. As the water plunges into the depths, a mist starts to rise from the floor of the valley. White, swirling clouds thicken as they ascend, until all but the Amethyst Mountain is obliterated from view.

The roar of the water is deafening, and eddies of a light breeze lift the spray until the mist envelopes you like a garment, small globules of moisture clinging to your hair and robe.

Chiron shouts above the clamor, "Look!" You follow his pointing finger to where, within the chasm of vapor, a rainbow manifests. Slowly, it travels upwards, becoming ever brighter, until it forms an arch of beauty over the mountain. One color glows more brightly than the rest. "See!" exclaims Chiron, "That is the color which harmonizes with your present level of development."

As he speaks, you are conscious of an answering tremor of response from your astral body. Although experienced on a personal level, the recognition of the power and vastness of the forces of life fills you with awe and you draw nearer to Chiron's steaming flanks.

"Come, enough is enough for one day." He draws you away from the brilliance and moves behind the rocks.

"Close your eyes and I will take you back to the place where you began this journey." He lifts you up, and in no time at all, you are back in the jungle. Chiron places you gently upon the ground.

"Sleep, now. I will be here when you return—and always." You murmur your thanks to him, as your eyes close on that friendly, bearded face.

Take time to adjust to your normal surroundings. This visualization has been the longest, so far, and may have tired you a little. So, have something to eat and drink, and relax. Leave a candle burning upon the altar for your friends on the inner planes.

CAPRICORNUS

DECEMBER 22ND–JANUARY 19TH

Planet: Saturn
Jewel: Garnet
Number: 8
Governs: Knees, Skin,
　　　　　Skeletal system

Color: Black
Metal: Lead
Flower: Hyacinth
Herb: Comfrey

Positive Traits
Ambitious; prudent; patient; contained; persevering.

Negative Traits
Pessimistic; miserly; over-exacting; rigid; a wet blanket;
self-deluded.

CAPRICORNUS

CAPRICORNUS

Midst towers of black and restless sky,
the Horned One rests in nature's byre;
heeds not our death lament, nor cry,
awaiting Star Child's light and fire.
The task complete and work well done,
Earth's crawling creatures shown the way,
to progress through the mill of life,
emerging better for the play.
One cycle o'er with more to come,
break chains that bind to present form;
with Karma purged and new life won,
and rebirth through the Gate of Horn.

LEON G. DICKENS

CAPRICORNUS

Capricornus is the third earth sign and the fourth cardinal sign of the zodiac. It is ruled by the slow-moving planet, Saturn, the Taskmaster of the zodiac.

Capricornus is a goat with a fish tail, showing that life originated in the sea. Another symbol is the agile Chamois, which climbs nimbly up the craggy slopes of the mountain.

As the ruler of Capricornus, Saturn represents Father Time, and souls born in this sign reach the top of their professions or occupations in the later years of life. Saturn prefers the not so young!

In the Cabbalistic Tree of Life, Saturn equates with the Great Mother, from whose womb comes all life. The color of this Sephera is black, and as this sign is feminine and of cardinal earth, the concept is entirely satisfactory.

The followers of Plato called this constellation the Gate of the Gods, through which the soul ascended to heaven. The Orientals knew it as the Southern Gate of the Sun, while the Latin poets named it the Rain-bringing One.

The Goat climbs step-by-step, but gets there, eventually. He is never distracted from his goal, but keeps looking ahead in the same direction. At the top of the sacred mountain, the Sun, at the Winter Solstice, shines on the achievements of Capricornus, in the valley that holds his past. From now on, the Sun will become warmer, and the days longer.

Souls born under this rulership, or having it strongly emphasized in their natal charts, will take life, and its attendant troubles, very seriously indeed. And the position of Saturn in a chart will reveal the lessons to be learned—the negative karma—which, according to house and position, must be discharged.

Souls of this sign can be relied upon in any eventuality. They hardly ever become flustered or excited, neither do they indulge in tantrums. But, beware, when anger *is* evoked and they consider a wrong has been perpetrated! The earth will move in more ways than one! It would be best, particularly if you are the cause of such anger, to give them a wide berth. They are an authority to themselves and justice will be meted out quite dispassionately.

They are, more often than not, "born old," and even in youth they hardly ever act in an impulsive manner, having a healthy respect for authority and the law in particular. Not for them, the devil-may-care kind of attitude. A rule is there to be obeyed, and they will not tolerate anyone who laughs in the face of the law.

Of course, this makes them excellent people to have in charge of a group or society. They will see to it that all the necessary by-laws and regulations are recognized and observed. Organization and efficiency are the keywords for this sign, and others may find it difficult to live up to these ideals. But, order must be kept in all areas of the community, and Capricornus is the sign of government at the highest levels.

These souls may have a tricky or awkward childhood and they themselves may sometimes be the cause of this. Because some parents do not understand the serious, melancholy child they have bred, and often force it, "for its own good," to enter into situations which are entirely foreign to its nature.

The soul is happiest when it is studying and learning—working with the utmost perseverance and concentration. Children are apt to irritate, so this sign has few, if any, offspring of its own.

As it climbs steadily onwards, and passes the less well endowed on the way, it is not improbable for a grim chuckle to issue from the lips of this diligent soul. The sense of humor is of a dark, saturnian quality.

The soul moves on through life, knowing, with an inner certainty, that the best is yet to come; that Saturn will bring all the rewards in the years of maturity. And, hidden within the deep wells of the spirit, the light, which has long been jealously guarded, will finally be displayed for all to see. The Priest-Initiate comes into his own and becomes the focus of power, love and wisdom. This sign is known as the Gate of the Gods. *Capricornus symbolizes consolidation.*

Legends

Assyro-Babylonian

Ea was a prominent god of the Assyro-Babylonian pantheon. Portrayed as a goat, with a fishtail, he was, perhaps, the original source of the Capricornus symbol. One of a triad of gods, his consort was the goddess Ninki or Damkina, the Great Spouse of the Lord.

Ea was the ruler of the waters and his name means "House of the Water," but this divinity is not to be confused with the sea. His sphere of influence covered the springs and great rivers, and stretches of fresh water.

In Sumer, he was known as Enki, Lord of the Earth, and held in awe as the god of supreme wisdom. His was the gift of prophesy and magical incantations, and thus he was invoked as an oracle, manifesting through the priest or shaman. Another of his titles was that of Lord of the Sacred Eye, the eye in question being the Third Eye, which gives clear sight.

Ea lived in the holy city of Eridu on the Persian Gulf, and Eridu was the first city to be built above the waters. The God's dwelling was the *Ezuab*, or the House of the Apsu and in the garden there grew a miraculous tree, a black *Kishkanu*. The tree's foliage cast a dense shadow, the color of lapis-lazuli.

A very ancient text states that Ea was regarded as the Creator in that he fashioned man from clay, in his own image.

Greek

The most popular association with Capricornus is the Goat-god, Pan. There is a mystery surrounding his birth because no one is sure who his parents were. His father is said to have been Hermes, but, as Pan is considered to be the foster-brother of Zeus, he would be far older than Hermes!

His mother has been variously mentioned as Dryope, daughter of Dryops; Penelope, wife of Odysseus; the nymph, Oeneis; and Amaltheia, the Goat.

Another source states that Pan was the son of Cronus and Rhea, which implies that he was around long before the classical gods of Greece came into being.

Pan lived and was worshipped in many places, including Arcadia, the most mountainous region of Greece. He was the god of shepherds and was a shepherd, himself, looking after flocks and herds and also the beehives. In fact, he was the god of all the inhabitants of the countryside.

In appearance, he was, to say the least, highly unusual. Two small horns crowned his head, his nose was flat and his nether parts were those of a goat, complete with tail. According to Homer, his nurse was a nymph called Sinoe, but as she was unable to come to terms with his looks, she fled and left him. However, he was cared for by the gods, themselves, and thus grew to maturity.

Pan was the inventor of the Pan-pipes, which had seven reeds. He named the instrument the Syrinx, after a beautiful girl of the same name, whom he desired. He attempted to violate this chaste maiden, but she escaped him by changing into a reed by the waters of the River Ladon. Unable to distinguish Syrinx from all the other reeds, he picked seven at random and made them into pipes.

Being the god of fecundity, Pan seduced many nymphs of the woods and mountains. He had a son, Iynx, by Echo, and another by Eupheme, called Crotus, who became the Bowman of the zodiac. Pan was fortunate enough to captivate the goddess, Selene, and gained her favors by transforming himself into a marvelous white ram.

Pan's most important festival was the *Lyceus*, a time of orgiastic revelry, when the god gave oracles on Mount Mycaea. In Rome, his festival was named the Lupercalia, and was celebrated on the 14th of February. A temple to Pan stood at the base of the Acropolis in Athens. In a suitably rustic setting, it was built in front of a natural cave in the rock face. It was founded because a runner, on his way to Athens, was accosted by Pan. The god asked the runner why a temple to Pan had not been erected in the city, and sent word to the authorities to build one. His request was granted!

At the exact time of the birth of Christianity, a sailor, one Thamus, heard a great voice calling over the Ionian Sea, "Thamus, are you there? When you reach Palodes, take care to proclaim that the great god Pan is dead!" Needless to say, this message was greeted with much grief and sorrow. But Pan—the embodiment of

Nature—can never die. As the saying goes, the old gods are not dead—they think *we* are!

Today, as in times past, people are again recognizing that the Divine manifests in everything that lives on the planet Earth. The life-giving forces embodied in Pan are inseparable from the Godhead—by whatever name it is known.

Egyptian

In ancient Egypt, the god named Consentes by the Romans had the same characteristics as Pan and ranked in position before all other gods. He was worshipped, with the greatest devotion, all over the land and considered to be the First Principle—the giver of all life. As a god of fecundity, his horns symbolized the rays of the Sun and his animated features—the brightness of the heavens.

Consentes wore a star upon his breast, depicting the universe and the spiritual part of his nature, while his shaggy, lower regions disclosed the link with the natural world. Thus, the god expressed the unity of all things.

The image of the goat was very prominent in the town of Mendes, which means "goat." The Goat of Mendes was a sacred animal, and, far from being the embodiment of all evil, it was regarded as a symbol of fertility. Great lamentations arose when the goat died, but it was soon replaced by another, and, like all the sacred animals in the Egyptian pantheon, it continued to be the focus of ceremonial worship.

The god, Min, was also identified with Pan. He, too, linked with fertility, and in representations he is seen wearing a crown and carrying a flail in his right hand. Like Pan, he was usually portrayed with an erect phallus and recognized as the Giver of Life.

Min was the god of vegetation and the protector of crops, and many temple wall paintings depict scenes from rituals conducted in his honor. As a harvest god, at the time of the king's enthronment, Pharaoh offers Min the first sheaf of corn, cut with his own hands.

In the classical era, this god was revered in Coptos, the town of caravaneers, where expeditions departed for commercial ventures. Before embarking upon their travels, the leaders of these expeditions always invoked the aid and protection of Min, who was the guardian of the Eastern desert and "Lord of foreign lands."

Min was also worshipped in Akhmin, originally known as Chemmis. The Greeks knew Akhmin as Panopolis and recognized the similarities between this god and Pan. Min's origins go back to the earliest part of history, when his sign—a thunderbolt—was carved upon the clan totem.

The Rite of Capricornus

Perform the rite at the Winter Solstice, or soon after the Sun has been reborn through the Horns of Capricornus. Prepare the altar and light a black (or dark brown) candle. A period of contemplation on the following theme introduces this rite.

One aspect of Capricornus and its ruler, Saturn, is that of time and age and the knowledge that we, as humans, occupy a mere fraction of eternity from birth to death. Yet here, at the Winter Solstice, we have the regeneration of the Sun, which speaks most forcibly of rebirth and renewal.

Look back on your past with its successes, failures, hopes and mistakes. Certain landmarks will stand out as peaks of victory, others as deep valleys, of sorrow and despair. But the soul continues climbing to the top of the mountain.

Joy and sorrow are the two sides of the same coin and we must learn to greet them both with a modicum of reserve. Recognize the impermanence of situations, and know that all things must eventually pass away.

A philosophical attitude to life needs to be nurtured. Even when we are in the midst of happiness, and enjoying it to the full, as we should, the higher self will be aware that all experience is but a learning process.

Capricornus is concerned with many things, and one of them is the sanctity of the Earth. In ancient times, the Earth was revered as a Mother Goddess, on whose breast we were sustained, and in whose loving arms we were received at our death. This primordial concept was worldwide and is being renewed in the present day. More and more people are appreciating the need to protect the Earth and everything upon it, at the time of its greatest peril.

Already, it has been suggested that the Earth is a living entity in its own right, a great organism which is self-controlling, sustaining and regulating both its own life and those of the tiny organisms that live upon its surface. Certain unorthodox scientists are the founders of this revolutionary theory, and have named it the Gaia Hypothesis, after Gaia, the Earth Mother of ancient Greece.

Of course, this theory is diametrically opposed to the commonly accepted idea, namely, that life occurred because conditions were conducive to its coming into being.

Certainly to live and exist in harmony with Gaia is of the greatest importance. Since time began, there have been rituals and festivals to this end because we knew, instinctively, that we must in some way make recompense for the miracle.

This we did, first with human or animal sacrifices, and later, as we developed, with the ritual of returning sheaves of corn and libations of wine to the Mother of All Living. From the smallest village custom, to the great fire festivals of the pagans and the witches, the nature year has been observed, marked, and acknowledged throughout history, down to the present day. And by sanctifying nature in this manner, we also sanctify and purify ourselves.

And now, gaze above the flame of the candle. Gradually, your eyes close, and you awaken in your visualization on the inner planes.

♑ ♑ ♑ ♑

You are sitting in the entrance of a small cave, and it is very cold. Outside, the snow is falling in large, thick flakes, onto an already white carpet that stretches into the distance. It is difficult to see anything clearly, but you sense the immense tranquillity of this place.

Nothing happens, so you stand up and notice a woolen robe at your feet. Thankfully, you don the warm garment, pulling the hood over your head and securing the robe with a rope girdle. You also discover a pair of soft, lined boots, and sink your feet into them with a sigh of relief.

Thus arrayed, you step out into the snowy landscape and peer around. As you stand there, you hear the faint sound of cowbells, and presently glimpse a long, thin line of bobbing lights moving slowly in your direction. As they approach, you can just make out that the lights are lanterns held aloft on poles, by a company of hooded figures. Animals, in the form of yaks, bear bundles on their backs and accompany the procession.

They pass by, walking steadily, without speaking or acknowledging your presence. You decide to follow at a discrete distance, but find it quite difficult to keep up with them, despite the ready-made path in the snow.

Your quickened breath hangs vaporized in the cold air as you struggle along in the footsteps of these travelers. Soon, there is a definite, though gradual ascent, leading to a range of dark mountains which rise into jagged peaks. You long to sink down in the snow and rest, but resist the impulse and push on with grim determination.

Now you are in the shelter of the rock-face and find that the lights have gone! Hurrying, you see the tracks disappear into an opening—a narrow fissure—that runs through the sheer sides of the living rock. Here a flickering light can be seen some way ahead, and walking is easier.

At last you emerge under a clear, star-bright sky. The scene before you is bathed in moonlight and makes you catch your breath. You have come to a valley protected by the mountains. The short turf is starred with flowers that grow everywhere; climbing the rocks and peeping over high ledges. A stream runs, chuckling and bubbling through this valley, and you can discern the goat-like chamois, leaping agilely among the crags and perching confidently on tiny protuberances.

The valley is alive with chanting voices. The procession you followed is only one of many. From every direction move lines of Buddhist monks, their lanterns creating a fairyland vista of twinkling lights. All the monks are making their way to a temple situated in the center of the valley. You can hear the deep reverberations of a gong hanging in the still air near the temple. Slowly, you begin to walk in the same direction, drawn to this mysterious place.

One by one, the monks enter the sacred precinct of the temple, first tethering the animals to convenient posts and removing their footwear. The heavy aroma of incense is powerful as you move to look inside the building. It is ablaze with light from hundreds of candles. In your turn, you climb the steps and dutifully leave your boots on the terrace with all the others.

Many hundreds of monks are gradually filling the vast interior of the temple. They seat themselves facing the statue of a gigantic, golden Buddha, which reposes in the customary lotus position, a slight enigmatic smile upon its features.

You sit down with the assembly, cross-legged and in the lotus position—if you can manage it! Almost immediately, you are calm and attentive to the atmosphere which is charged with spiritual power. The chanting continues, and the smoke from the incense curls upwards in never-ending spirals.

In spite of the number present, it is comfortably cool within the temple. And quite suddenly, you realize that this vast assembly is meditating upon the whole of humanity! The thoughts of these monks are being concentrated into one great effort in order to bring more harmony into the world. In a sense, it is as though they are acting as nurse to the Earth by sending forth rays of comfort and healing to our planet and to the life upon it.

You willingly join with them in this work, and soon, a cone of golden radiance builds above the statue of the Buddha. It glows ever brighter, until a perfect pyramid of white luminosity hovers in the air. Abruptly, the chanting ceases and the shining cone vanishes, as though plucked out of existence. The power has been transmuted.

Now, the atmosphere is flat and ordinary and the monks slowly file out of the temple. You feel a tug at your sleeve, and one of the monks smiles and beckons. You retrieve your footwear and follow him, breathing the fresh mountain air and watching the newborn sun's first rays creeping over the grass.

Crossing the stream by way of large stones set strategically in the fast-flowing water, your companion makes for the opposite cliffs and the dark opening of a cave. He turns and smiles reassuringly, then dives into the entrance.

Inside, you traverse a passage lit by flaring torches, and soon daylight shows again. The monk indicates that you are to proceed alone, then bows, and is gone.

In front of you, the landscape is green and flat with circular huts dotted here and there. Several well-worn paths meander through the long grass, and the only visible movement is lazy smoke, curling from the tops of the huts. You notice that some areas of the land are surrounded by rough fences made from thin slices of wood, bound together with reeds. Away to the right, a gleam of water reveals a marshy tract, so you choose a path that skirts the huts and walk quietly along in the early morning sun.

Small stones are spaced at intervals along this path. They are covered with many diverse symbols such as butterflies, trees, pillars, and magical signs that include a triangle, painted blue.

The path twists and turns upon itself, only to resume its original direction further on. Now the huts are left behind, and you are approaching two stone pillars, carved with breast-like cupolas, that stand before an enclosure which is protected by a low stone wall.

You walk between the pillars, aware that you have entered a sacred place, and also aware that this is one of the most solitary journeys you have taken!

But now, the gentle lowing of cattle is heard, and there, in the center of the enclosure, stands a large round byre. The bright eyes of calves peep through sturdy reed-woven walls, but your attention is riveted by the stone figure which stands at the doors of the byre.

The Mother Goddess sits with a child, half-animal, half-human, at her breast, and regards you steadily with the hint of a smile curving her lips. Her hair is dressed in a high-standing style, topped by a crown of gleaming jet. Both the Goddess and her child wear necklaces of pearly-white globular beads.

In front of the byre, a great crescent of white stones extends like embracing arms. This is the Gate of Horn, denoting sacred land where gods and men unite.

A rustling turns your head, just in time to glimpse someone disappearing behind one of the pillars. A basket of food has been brought for you! Thankfully, you sit down in the shelter of the wall and tuck into coarse bread and figs, quenching your thirst from two stone jugs, one containing water, and the other, milk. Even though this is one of the loneliest journeys, it appears that you are watched over!

Then, something else happens. The stillness is broken in a most agreeable manner by the thin fluting of pipes—a melody, haunting and sweet. And there, sitting nonchalantly on the wall of the enclosure, is the unmistakable figure of Pan! With pipes at his lips and shaggy goat-foot limbs at ease, the god of all nature caresses the reeds with nimble fingers.

Slanting, amber eyes gaze over the grasslands—his heritage—his, by right, as keeper and shepherd of the wild things. The Great God Pan keeps you company while you rest. Then, raising a hand in farewell, he leaps from the wall and is gone.

You save some bread and liquid as an offering to the Goddess and approach the statue. You scatter crumbs, and as a libation, pour the remains of the water and the milk onto the ground.

She is very life-like and you are comforted by her presence here. The Goddess broods over the land and seems to lend contentment to the animals within their enclosure, which apart from an occasional bleat and snuffle, are quiet and at peace in their environment.

You look up into the strange, bird-like eyes. This stone carving of a mother and child externalizes our oldest ideas of divinity, embracing the concept of Earth as mother and nurse, the source of all creation.

You put out your hands and touch the cool knees, huge and rounded. A feeling of calm steals over you, and, sitting down, you rest your head at the Mother's feet.

You can hear your heartbeat thudding in your ears. Boom, boom, boom, the sound fills your consciousness like a muffled drum. But, is it your *heart*, or something else? Boom, boom, boom. It creates an hypnotic effect, quieting, but at the same time disturbing.

You become aware of a presence. Opening your eyes, you are confronted by someone in a filmy, gray robe. The figure stands near you, a swathing of the gauze-like material concealing the features. It emits strong, benign rays of power which are almost tangible. Raising its arms, the filmy robe shimmers with starlight, as though the material has transformed into a night sky! Slowly, you are drawn into its folds and lifted into the air.

In no time at all, you can feel the earth again beneath your feet. A dark, sloping tunnel opens in front of you, and light from occasional flares reveal the gray-robed figure some way ahead. The ground is very uneven and a strong smell of dank earth mixed with the odor of dried blood becomes more intense with every uncertain step you take.

At one point, water gushes from a cavity and accompanies you, running down a groove on one side of the tunnel. At last, you stumble into a huge cave where the blackness is held at bay by more torches, secured to the walls. Here, the smell of blood and decay is overpowering!

The floor of the cave is strewn with bleached bones and bits of animal skins, and across at the far side stands a gigantic figure carved from the living rock and still attached to it at the back.

The naked woman is blackened by smoke and smeared with the blood of many sacrifices. She is seated with hands folded across her belly, but the head of the women is wreathed in darkness where the flickering flares cannot reach.

More primitive and coarse than the Goddess of the Byre, she exudes a primeval force which fills the whole cave and gives a feeling of apprehension. The place is crowded with the astral shells of dead animals—a dreadful place, indeed!

The gray-robed figure is standing at the side of the statue and her presence is reassuring. But, if only someone would speak!

"I will speak to you, now." The figure draws back its veil to reveal the face of an old, old woman, yet the voice gives no indication of old age.

"The sign of Capricornus is one of brooding silence, of darkness before the dawn, and death before rebirth. It is of the rocks and the dark reaches of space, whence all life comes. Its essence is time, which each life-form views in a different and special way—ranging from the butterfly, whose life-span is one or two days, to that of a star, which can be millions of years. In the end, time is irrelevant, of interest only to the manifest world.

"The life span of your world is governed by Saturn, who is known as Father Time, and sometimes, Death. You have some knowledge of that gentleman, but he merely regulates and measures the ratio of energy and atoms, whether in or out of manifestation. There is really nothing frightening in all this.

"Energy, in the form of light, can never be destroyed, and so it is with souls or sparks from the ineffable Godhead.

"My name is Hecate, and this is my province. I guide lost souls and bring all to the Mother, of whom I am an aspect. You have seen the fertile Mother with her animals, but now you are looking upon Black Isis, one of the earliest concepts of the Goddess. This sanctuary was made in her honor, and the life she gave so willingly was returned at certain times, as a thanksgiving for *that* fertility. It was the highest form of worship and the most selfless. Black Isis is the giver of dynamic force—the primordial essence whence life itself, began."

You look again at the crude, sensual carving; the streak of soot lying across the heavy breasts, the great thighs set slightly apart, and the vast belly holding new life. You begin to tremble, and your heart goes out to that venerable giantess.

Then, a strange thing occurs. The beating, as of a great heart, begins again and fills the cave as though it were the body of a living being. With each thud, an answering flood of life-force pervades your body, until you can bear it no longer, and, stumbling forward, you fall against the statue, your arms reaching out to clasp the huge limbs.

Your tears darken the stone and trickle down the slab-like legs. Here, in the womb of the Earth, communing with the fructifying powers of nature, a great peace envelopes you.

"It is time to go." The voice of Hecate intrudes. Straightening up, you gasp at her appearance. Gone are the wrinkles and the gray, straggly hair. They have been replaced by a smooth, milky complexion and honey-colored tresses, cascading about her shoulders.

A gentle smile touches the full, red lips, "Everything is change," says she. "I may be young or old as I please. Now you see me as the young moon."

She beckons with a slender, white hand and disappears through a narrow fissure in the rock. You follow, with a last glance at Black Isis.

Another passage is negotiated which eventually leads to a series of caves. The atmosphere becomes steadily colder until you can see an entrance and the falling snow, outside.

"I have brought you back to where you began this journey. I will always be near at hand." The Goddess opens her arms and embraces you. "Be brave and continue upon the Path . . . and come back soon."

The Goddess waits while you take off the warm robe and the boots, then, as you sit down, the scene begins to fade.

In the familiar surroundings of your room, observe the usual procedure and leave a lighted candle upon the altar.

AQUARIUS

JANUARY 20TH–FEBRUARY 18TH

Planet: Uranus
Jewel: Amethyst
Number: 4
Governs: Calves, Ankles

Color: Sky Blue
Metal: Platinum
Flower: Snowdrop
Herb: Mullein

Positive Traits
A humanitarian; independent; friendly; original; inventive; a reformer.

Negative Traits
Unpredictable; eccentric; contrary; rebellious.

AQUARIUS

In the darkness of the void
brightly shines a single flame
as the Goddess, but a maiden
spawns the snowdrop in her name.

The Goddess, now the Star Child
fulfilling Eostra's law
rouses nature to her task
with misted fling of golden spore.

The Gates of Avatar stand open
as is poured upon the Earth
libation from the Virgin, for
Revival and Rebirth.

Uranus in his airy kingdom
his major planets seven;
inventive, bold, with changing helm,
gives freedom from the heaven.

And Sirius, Guardian of the Light
Oh! guiding star of seer and sage,
foretells that we redeem ourselves
within the new Aquarian age.

JEANNE D. DICKENS

AQUARIUS

Aquarius is the third air sign and the fourth fixed sign of the zodiac. It is ruled by Uranus, known as the Magician of the Zodiac, because this planet is the transformer and has a fervour for change and innovation.

The sign depicts a man pouring water from two urns, but in the earliest representations, a woman was thus portrayed. The water is more satisfactorily interpreted as steam or vapor, having been transmuted and fixed by this final air sign—or air in resolution.

Before the discovery of Uranus in 1781, Aquarius was considered to be governed by Saturn, and even today, it is sometimes given the double rulership of both Saturn and Uranus. But Aquarius is so obviously connected with the revolutionary, the new and unusual, that Uranus must always have been the sign's natural ruler, although only recently discovered.

The Water Bearer pours the *aqua nostra* or Waters of Life and Renewal, down upon the Earth at the beginning of the new year. In occultism, the twin streams are seen as blood and water and represent the magico-mystical energies—the magnetic fluids of new life. They are intimately connected with the mysteries of Maat—the Star Goddess—the star in question being Sirius, and having thirteen points.

Aquarius is the reformer, the innovator and the great transformer. The sign is known as the brotherhood of man and this characteristic is blended with an interest in humanity as a whole. Like the vapor from the urns, it is spread far and wide, for Aquarius is friend to all the world.

Every 2,145 years, or thereabouts, the Sun appears to slip backwards into another sign of the sidereal zodiac. This astronomical event, known as the precession of the equinoxes, is due to a slight wobble in the rotation of the Earth, much like that of a spinning top which is running down. It is calculated at the Vernal Equinox from the position of the Sun on the equator, in relation to the Pole Star. The Pole Star is the guiding factor in this phenomenon.

The equinoctial point is now nearing the constellation of Aquarius and occultists assert that at such prestigious time, the character and spirit of the new sign impinges on our consciousness and results in revolutionary changes of thought which influence every sphere of existence. At this point in time, Aquarius shines as a beacon in the zodiac, illuminated by the Sun's rays and with *that* star's tremendous power drawing forth the sign's qualities.

The discovery of Uranus by William Herschel in 1781 was significant. At that time, the Earth received the macrocosmic rays of Aquarius through its true rule, Uranus. However one views the matter, in terms of evolution, a scientific breakthrough quickly followed the discovery—with the invention of radio, television, space travel and aeronautics.

When Uranus was discovered and was seen to be in existence in 1781, the planet announced that the time was right for new inventions and new knowledge. In this way, the stars and planets could act as a gigantic clock; the spheres working in harmony on a continuing, expanding spiral. In future ages, new planets will be found *at the right time* to herald yet more advanced forms of expansion, totally incomprehensible to the world in its present stage of development.

The Age of Pisces has held sway for the last 2,145 years and is now giving ground to the Age of Aquarius. The death pangs of Pisces and of the Piscean influence is apparent to all with eyes to see. The wind of Aquarius is blowing away the established order of things and all previously conceived ideologies and concepts of a Piscean nature. Certain it is that Pisces, the sign of mutable water, is very different from Aquarius, the sign of fixed air. In the light of this knowledge, it is to be hoped that the transition will take place without too much conflict!

Aquarius grants universal consciousness and already a truly alchemical change is occuring, with social and religious dogmas being rapidly discarded.

In the field of science, it has been discovered that an atom can be split and that such a procedure yields enormous energy. It is, therefore, realized that the old idea of a material world, fixed and unchanging, is no longer valid — and matter is now viewed as an aspect of energy. Occultists have always maintained that matter is brought into being from the unmanifest, the source of all power, and that the whole globe thrills with vibrations from the unseen fields of cosmic space.

In the New Age, the crossing of all boundaries, social, cultural and spiritual, is to be expected and welcomed. Aquarius represents unity. The blurring of all frontiers will become the accepted norm, together with the accompanying transcendence of the spirit. Occult sciences, including such things as telepathy and thought transference, will be incorporated into everyday life. Already, some scientists are seriously investigating the paranormal and have proved the validity of many borderline energies hitherto thought of as "bunk."

Souls born under Aquarius have a big part to play, both in the present day and in the coming years. They, more than others, are concerned with humanity as a whole and have the necessary innate sympathy for their brethren which can go a long way in establishing a rapport between the cultures and races of the world. Those born with Aquarius strongly emphasized in their natal charts will also be called upon to serve the spirit of the New Age.

Aquarians can incur hostility through an absence of sentiment. This is because the soul is orientated on a broader humanitarian level which rises above personal relationships. Nevertheless, when an Aquarian friend makes contact after a year's absence, he or she is often puzzled by the coolness of response and the apparent lack of understanding!

Once the mind is made up, the soul will pursue its goal, despite any opposition or criticism, and herein lies the sign's chief stumbling-block. The soul may view its opinions as infallible and continue upon an unwise course. It is then that the lightning flash of Uranus strikes with deadly accuracy across the seemingly ordered life pattern. All preconceived ideas and 'ologies are consumed in the fire of purification, and while it may appear that the darkest day has dawned, this is far from the truth. The purging that ensues leaves no choice but to make a complete break with the past and to start afresh. Loss of some kind is a certainty, but when all has been assimilated, the dispassionate and reasoning qualities of this soul aid it to achieve perspective, and from then on, troubles are viewed in a more altruistic manner.

Through suffering, the heart center, from the opposite, complimentary sign of Leo, is awakened and balanced with this far-seeing mind. The result is an individual of true Aquarian caliber who will lovingly work for the benefit of all. Like the hero in the myth, the soul has faced the "dark night" and has emerged victorious. Now, the Aquarian can truly bear the life-giving substance of the Urns and give to those less well-endowed the comfort of solace and healing. Synthesis between body, mind and soul is the hallmark of the Aquarian Age. This sign is known as Cosmic Solidarity. *Aquarius symbolizes universal brotherhood.*

Legends

Assyro-Babylonian

In this part of the world, the Earth-Mother had many names such as Bau, Innini, Ga-Tum-Dug, Ninkhursag and Gula. They all represented the Great Goddess, the creative principle.

Gula was the Babylonian name for Aquarius, and this goddess, known as the Great Doctoress, was associated with childbirth and healing. It is similar to Western tradition, where the goddess as Bride is celebrated as the goddess of childbirth and healing, and where her festival of Imbolc occurs in the sign of Aquarius!

A scene depicted upon an Assyrian chalcedony seal and dated 990 to 600 B.C., shows Gula floating in the air. She wears a tiara and a long pleated skirt and she supports a winged disc which hovers above her head. At either side of her figure, two vases are seen in the heavens. They pour down twin streams of water which are received by two similar vases on the earth. Two male winged figures are in attendance and each hold a vessel thought to contain lustral water.

The idea of lustration and of cleansing, on all levels of existence, is very forcibly expressed by the sign of Aquarius, which also reveals the time of year these activities should be observed.

Another aspect of the goddess was Bau, who was the daughter of the God, Anu, and who breathed new life into human beings. Annually, on New Year's Day, her solemn nuptials were celebrated. In the midst of her worshippers, the goddess was led into the bridal chamber and prepared for her husband. She was given many gifts in order to ensure fertility, not only for herself, but also for her people. In the course of time, she became the mother of septuplet virgins.

Most probably, the role of the goddess would be enacted by a girl who was both chaste and beautiful—someone worthy to be her earthly representative. Like the Celtic Bride, the rituals praised a virgin goddess who would one day be called mother.

Greek
In Greek mythology, Ganymede had charge of the Waters of Heaven as he was thought of as the deity whose duty it was to sprinkle the Earth with rain. Indeed, many of the ancient astronomers rightly or wrongly identified him with Aquarius, the Water Bearer.

Ganymede was of human origins, but authorities differ as to his parentage. The most popular theory is that he was the son of Tros, King of Phrygia, and of Callirrhoe. His appearance was one of exceptional beauty and he was usually depicted as a young man wearing a Phrygian cap, with a cloak hanging loosely from his elegant white shoulders.

Zeus became enamored of the beautiful youth, and taking the form of an eagle, he carried Ganymede to Olympus. The young man became the favorite of Zeus and was given the position of Cup-bearer to the gods. Thus, his immortality was assured, and by way of compensation, Zeus presented his father with a team of magnificent horses, swift as the storm. Ganymede was revered at Sicyon and at Phlius.

Ancient Persian
In the mythology of ancient Persia, there is reference to the goddess, Anahita, who was the goddess of waters, fecundity and procreation. She was well-loved and widely venerated in this part of the world. Anahita became associated with Mithras and was later known throughout Asia Minor under the Hellenistic name of Anaaitis.

North American
The American Indians worship the Earth-Mother who sanctifies the ground with the Water of Life. The great tribe of the Algonquins call her Nokomis, the Grandmother.

The Rite of Aquarius

Perform the rite when the Sun has entered the sign of Aquarius. Prepare your altar in the usual way and light a pale blue candle. Begin by contemplating the essence of the sign in the following manner:

While Capricornus looks to the past, Aquarius encompasses the future and represents extension. It is the sign of starry space and the New Age will force us to free ourselves in more ways than one! Already, we are reaching for the stars and have earned the right to move into stellar space and become Children of the Stars.

Our oldest dream of traveling to the Moon is already achieved, and in future times the Moon will be colonized, with many souls being reborn upon that orb, in a suitably contrived atmosphere. Visiting and documenting Earth's neighboring planets will be commonplace as we travel deeper into the universe.

Extension will also occur on inner levels. Telepathy, clairvoyance and ESP will be accepted as natural abilities, moving towards super consciousness. With all this as the norm, psychic awareness will be treated in a rational manner and recognized for what it is—a most important part of the human condition.

Sit back in your chair and relax your body. Your mind is very alert as you gaze at the aura of the candle-flame. Close your eyes and prepare to visualize a new journey.

≈   ≈   ≈   ≈

You are resting comfortably on solid ground. Around you, the grass is long and grows in waving sheaves, and the only sounds are the piping of small birds and the droning of an occasional bee, as it draws sweetness from the clover. There is no reason to move at the moment, so you merely rest on Mother Earth and absorb the peaceful atmosphere.

Presently, you roll over and discover that you are in the center of a stone circle. The great, gray fingers stand out against a clear sky in which the sun moves towards the distant horizon. You attempt to count the monoliths, but find it difficult, so you concentrate upon their individual shapes. All are roughly the same height, and as you feel an urge to touch them, you stand up and walk across the circle.

It is a large ring and is situated in softly, undulating pasture which stretches as far as the eye can reach. Feeling the surfaces of the stones, you sense that they are extremely friendly. Each one exudes an aura of well-being that intoxicates you and sends you off into gales of laughter, without quite knowing why!

Your hands move lovingly over the stones as you run and skip among them. Many are covered in moss and lichen, the subdued tones of green and gold blending delicately with the uniform grayness.

Quite out of breath, you sit down again to recover, and notice a great avenue of stones leading from the circle and marching away into the distance. Perhaps this is the way you should go? Perhaps! But you are loath to leave the circle. You look at all the stones and realize that they are pointing up to the heavens. They are indicating the starry sky!

The sun has almost set, and the stars show brilliantly now that their rival has left the stage. This sunset is one of the most exquisite you have ever witnessed. The colors are extremely vivid and change from the deepest shade of rose, through to lilac, and from bright orange to the palest yellow, in no time at all. It is a display worthy of the mystical realms and a consummation of Being in all its glory. Beauty is present whether in or out of incarnation. You observe nature—entranced.

Soon, the vast orange disc of a full moon begins to rise above the edge of the horizon. The sight fills you with a deep longing, for what you do not know. An unfulfilled need, perhaps, to be "at one" with nature—to be absorbed into this splendor. This longing is followed by a feeling of serenity, as your soul is fed at the Well of Life.

The moon rises steadily and fills the night with a golden radiance. It hangs over the stones, illuminating and benevolent. One upright seems to sway in ecstatic glee! But, surely, this is lunar enchantment?

At this sublime moment, a thick white mist begins to gather and curl round the bases of the dark sentinels. Slowly, slowly, it coils, like a great white serpent, rising ever higher, until only the tops of the pillars show above the pearly-white vapor. It undulates and moves, as if alive, covering the monoliths in billowing dresses of ethereal substance. You can only stare—fascinated.

Now, the stone fingers have completely vanished, and what was once a stone circle has become writhing columns of vapor. As you watch, the mist runs out along the ground until a new circle of whiteness is formed near the earth. The manifestation is repeated at the tops of the columns, then the two circles start to ripple in small waves—creating the glyph of Aquarius!

The twin streams of mystical, magnetic fluid surround you in waves of power! The transformation is accompanied by a humming sound, as of a generator. The earth beneath your feet starts to vibrate, trembling in sympathy and anticipation. It almost seems as if the circle of mist is about to lift off like a spacecraft! But there is no fear in your soul—merely a yearning for new knowledge on the path.

Then, the noise abates; the earth quietens once more, and from out of the mist comes shadowy figures who move forward to greet you. With smiling faces and outstretched arms, they approach until you are surrounded by an eager throng! In a variety of dress, they come from every part of the world; each one representing a race or culture. And although they speak in many diverse tongues, the language barrier is transcended through the dynamic double waves of power. The Magic Circle of Aquarius unites *all* in a universal brotherhood.

A Chinese lady with painted face and a Mexican man with flowing mustaches both vie for your attention. A fur-clad Eskimo chatters avidly to a graceful Indian girl, while an Aborigine and a kilted Scotsman converse earnestly together. Yet, despite this social intercourse between the peoples of the world, it is obvious that something more mysterious is happening at this meeting.

The electromagnetic influences of Aquarius are being brought to bear here. The minds and souls of all the people present are being prepared to receive the influx of new thought and awareness. You are conscious of tingling sensations in various areas of your body. The seven psychic centers, or chakras, the centers of energy, are being fed with *prana,* the life-force.

The chakras can be described as whirling wheels which are spaced out between the base of the spine and the crown of the head. They are closely linked with the astral body and can be seen by clairvoyants as vortices of light and color.

As they ascend the spine, each one vibrates at a higher frequency, until the crown is reached. At this moment, the consciousness of the people is being gently extended and the dross of the lower self is transmuted. Everyone senses this contact, and, as the interaction takes place, conversation is abandoned and silence descends upon the assembly. This is a precursory glimpse of what is to come for every soul on Earth.

The contact reaches a peak then slowly ebbs away and the attention is suddenly drawn to the avenue of marching stones. The glyph of Aquarius has parted to reveal the open countryside, and now everyone moves to pass through the gateway in the mist and follow the beckoning monoliths over the downs.

It is a pleasant walk, with the people strolling along in twos and threes under a high-flying moon. A strong breeze is picking up and carries the salty smell of the sea on its bosom. You glance back, and discover that the glyph has been blown away and once more the stone circle stands solidly on the plain.

The path begins to climb and the journey continues in a companionable atmosphere, the long procession resembling a huge serpent, winding through the tall stones.

Soon, the avenue reaches a high plateau, with the stones descending into the valley on the far side of the hill. Everyone stands together to contemplate the view from this vantage point. It is of immense proportions, with streams, rivers, hills and forests, illuminated in bright moonlight. In the far distance, the waves of the ocean catch the moonbeams in silvery sparks, as if to draw the radiance into the watery depths.

Individuals in the crowd point out landmarks, while others gaze at a sky ablaze with stars, as if searching for familiar constellations. You can see the stone avenue standing out in gray uniformity. It reaches level ground, skirts a wood, and finally terminates at the edge of a circular expanse of water. The lake mirrors the moon's image, and from this distance looks like an enormous looking-glass laid down by a giant.

The people settle into a quiet reverie and are content to commune with nature seen here in one of her calmer moods. You begin to wonder what other experiences lie in store on this night of nights! You have not long to wonder!

Even now, fingers are pointing to a mass of clouds which have appeared on the horizon. Building gradually into a great billowing, milk-white carpet, they advance across the sky, to hover over the landscape.

Through the clouds flash streamers of incandescent light in a myriad of spectrum colors—purple, rose, brilliant blue, verdant green, and in all the variations of shades possible. The splendor of the phenomenon is awesome, and some people kneel in prayer, while others hold out their arms in wonder and amazement. One or two hide their faces, as if unable to comprehend the dazzling sight. They are gently raised and reassured by the more advanced souls in the crowd.

Then, miraculously, a divine face emanates from the center of the clouds. The features are those of a woman, her long flowing hair and white shoulders glowing with effulgence. Through her transparent form, stars show, glinting and winking, and above her head are set the Sun's planets—a shimmering, whirling, crown of splendor.

The countenance of the Star Goddess is one of unearthly beauty as she looks down, a faint smile curling her lips. And as the sea of upturned faces observe the vision, a mystical union occurs between the Star Goddess and every soul on the plateau—a unique and personal communion to be treasured for all time.

At last, the lustrous eyes close for a moment, to indicate that the communion is at an end. And now, her shapely, white arms extend and in each hand is held a gleaming amphora, one of silver, the other of gold. Slowly, their contents are poured out and descend in sparkling showers of light. It is as though the very stars have been transformed into a mass of glittering grains which fall to earth—a stream of incandescence.

One of the showers meets the earth, spreading over hill and valley in a carpet of tiny flashing sparks. The other falls into the lake, turning the water into a shimmering phosphorescence. The scene resembles a fairy tale image of childhood dreams and fantasies.

The contents of the amphoras coalesce with the elements and are absorbed by them, until all appears as it was before. In the heavens, only the cotton-wool clouds remain, to remind those present of what has come to pass. Truly, the Earth, and all that lives upon it, has received the seeds of the new age, bestowed by the Star Goddess, Herself!

The company walks back down the hill, most of them unaware that each person carries a star-seed, winking skyward from the crown of their heads. And this, of course, includes you!

The seeds of the Aquarian Age will be assimilated and spread by each carrier to every race on Earth, eventually emerging as revolutionary thought-forms.

Soon, the stone circle is reached. When everyone is safely within its boundaries, the mist returns, and there are fond farewells as the people disappear into it to be re-united with their physical bodies. Alone, once more, you lie down and the astral scene gradually fades.

Sitting in front of your altar you immediately remember your very own star-seed! But, most of all, you remember the Star Goddess!

PISCES

FEBRUARY 19TH – MARCH 20TH

Planet: Neptune
Jewel: Aquamarine
Number: 7
Governs: Feet, Lymphatic
system

Color: Sea Green
Metal: Silver
Flower: Primrose
Herb: Meadowsweet

Positive Traits
Compassionate; sympathetic; emotional; sensitive; receptive.

Negative Traits
Vague; weak-willed; deceptive; extremely changeable.

PISCES

The dreaming orb in mystic flight,
in purple sky of waking fire,
so softly breathes her promise bright
on burning sea of our desire.

With Neptune's rise from wintry dark
to meet the Light of Life halfway,
the white-fanged snarl of forces mark
the clash of might, as dark meets day.

Earth's restless rule in tidal bore
doth twist and tremble in delight,
whilst bound by Nature's covert law
as Venus rules from lofty height.

In ovular mode, the Piscean fish
wildly whirl all senses drown,
with beauteous Spring, the lovers' wish
and Eostra dons her bridal gown.

LEON G. & JEANNE D. DICKENS

PISCES

Pisces is the third water sign and the fourth mutable sign of the zodiac. This culminating sign is governed by Neptune, one of the planets that is located on the outer edge of the solar system.

Neptune's influence gives a haunting, other-world quality. It blurs and smudges all defined areas, and the borders between the material and the ethereal dissolve completely. The ruler of Pisces reveals that body and soul are blended for the sake of evolutionary experience.

Pisces is depicted as two fishes, tied together by a cord, and swimming in opposite directions. Truly, it is one of the most complex of the twelve signs and is as changeable as the sea.

This is the sphere of dissolution, where the soul is attempting to throw off the shackles of incarnation and, therefore, the fetters of desire. It can be described as the Waters of Lethe (forgetfulness), mysteriously transcending time and space in its efforts to slip the ties of mortality, which are represented by the cord.

Each time the soul returns to Pisces on the evolutionary spiral, there is a deep longing for its true home—the realms of spirit. When life is over, and the waters of oblivion close over it, what joy, the soul experiences! The ancient Greeks declaimed:

> As old mythologies relate
> Some draught of Lethe doth await
> The slipping through from state to state.

Jupiter, the original ruler of Pisces, is benevolent in this sign, and anyone who has this planet in the sign of

Pisces in their natal chart is blessed with unconquerable faith. It also gives particularly pure psychic experiences, which, even in later years, remain extremely vivid in the memory. Jupiter in Pisces is an aspect of grace bestowed.

Pisces is full of contradictions and, like the ocean itself, can change according to the environment around it. As a sign of duality it is one of the most mysterious, and is as remote as the unknown depths of the sea.

The soul is extremely sensitive to atmosphere, and much feeling is poured out to the grief-stricken and all who suffer. Identifying with suffering is one of the qualities, and the pain is often absorbed into itself. With such intense feeling, combined with the gift of a strong imagination, the soul can become a mystic of the highest caliber.

In the young soul, there is usually a lack of direction in life and it can be drawn back and forth, here and there, by the attraction of the moment. Looking for—it knows not what!

There is a deep yearning to be loved and wanted, and here, the young soul can make some grave mistakes. It may see the loved one through a dreamy, romantic haze, and picture the person as a mythical hero or heroine. And this is all very well, if the adored one is of an understanding disposition. But when "flaws" begin to appear in the character of the beloved, the beautiful vision fades. And because the Piscean is not quite of this world, the flaws with which, alas, we are all endowed, are viewed as serious personality defects.

It is true to say that a long-term relationship is rarely experienced by the Piscean. The innate aura of sadness and disappointment with humanity as a whole is often present and lingers into old age. This is because the soul is finely tuned and is ever conscious of its links with more perfect planes of being.

The evolved soul in Pisces has inwardly turned away from the material world—the world of phenomena. More and more, it perceives the land of youth from whence it came, and the experiences hitherto gained are refined in this sign, so that only the essence remains.

The Piscean should beware of acting upon what is often clouded judgment. It is wise to be fully cognizant of all the facts in a situation before moving in any direction. One of the faults of the sign is hearing only what it *wants* to hear!

The negative aspects of Neptune foster an attraction for drugs and the desire to live in a world of fantasy, which, for the young soul, can be dangerous. On the positive side, however, we find that the muse-inspired poet, par excellence, is usually a Piscean! These souls can be vague, nebulous and often irritating, but at the same time, can act as mirrors in which we view ourselves!

The tremendous influence of mutable water makes out-of-the-body experiences the norm for some, while others have precognitive dreams of exceptional clarity.

For the advanced soul, working through this sign, there is an immense rapport with those less fortunate in the game of life. We find them in hospitals, charitable institutions, and wherever they can lighten the sufferings of others. Where indeed would we be without that most compassionate of individuals, the Piscean? This sign is known as the "Mystical Marriage." *Pisces symbolizes universal love.*

Legends

Greek

In Greece, no deity has more connection with the Fish than the Great Goddess. In one guise, that of St. Mary of Egypt, she is portrayed wearing a blue robe (symbolical of the sea), and a pearl necklace, the one constant adornment upon statues of the goddess. In this respect, it is very easy to equate the virgin with the ancient sea-goddess, Marian.

The names—Marian, Marianne (sea lamb), Myrtea and Mariana, all disclose her tutelary role as the Goddess from the Sea. So much so, that the mermaid came into being as a lovely fair-haired woman with a mirror (the symbol of Venus), and a comb of gold.

The goddess with the fish-tail passed down into legend and still holds a fascination for the young in heart. The merry-maid, or mermaid, is none other than Aphrodite, the love goddess, born from sea-foam. Her temples were raised near the water's edge, and Myrrh, the bittersweet herb of death, was burned to her. This signified that the underworld was also her province.

As *Stella Maris*, or Myrrh of the Sea, she is at once the exaltation of Pisces and the owner of the Magic Mirror that unites body and soul.

Roman

Venus and Cupid were so terrified by the giant, Typhon, that they plunged into the Euphrates river and turned themselves into fishes. But the goddess, Minerva, took pity on their plight and placed them in the heavens where mother and son became known as the sign of Pisces. Dovetailed together, they were assured of immortality, while the umbilical cord connects Venus (fertility), with Cupid (love).

Babylonian
Pisces was known to the Babylonians as Kun, or the Constellation of the Tails. The Fishes were also recognized as the Leash, to which were tied Anunitum and Simmah, two fish-goddesses.

Chaldean
The ancient Chaldeans had a lore in which the swallow-headed fish expressed the idea of psychic generation, and this is also the character for Pisces, the sign which speaks of rebirth through the waters of regeneration.

Syrian
In this part of the world, the goddess Derceto took the form of a fish. She was also known as Atargatis, and under this name was identified with Ishtar and Astarte. The latter goddess was intimately connected with water and fertility, and indeed, all the elements of earth and heaven.

At Eddessa, Ascalon, and Hierapolis, there were large fish ponds which were sacred to the goddess. The fish in these pools grew rapidly in size until they were of immense proportions. They were given special names, and when called, would swim up to the surface to be patted and given a titbit. The goddess Atargatis descended into the waters of the pool at Hierapolis. When she returned to heaven, she took with her two fishes which became the sign of Pisces.

Near Eastern
The religion of Judaism has much symbolism regarding fish. The partaking of fish on the eve of the Jewish Sabbath is well known. It is considered to be holy food and is eaten on a Friday, the day sacred to Venus.

The Jews also hold a belief regarding the end of the world. This concerns certain messiahs who will capture the Leviathan, a fabulous creature in the form of a fish, and give a portion of its flesh to each of the followers of that religion. The Leviathan is said to bear the weight of the world upon its back, in much the same way as Atlas.

The sacredness in which the fish was held also passed to the new religion of Christianity, where it became the symbol of Jesus the Christ, in the then new Age of Pisces.

When Christianity was declared the state'religion of Rome, and even before that time, pictures of fish were scratched upon every available wall and building and were especially prevalent in the catacombs beneath that city.

As the Greek word for fish is Ichthus, the early Christians utilized these characters to produce an ideograph of faith—Iesous CHristos, THeou Uios Soter: ICHTHUS (Jesus Christ, Son of God, Savior).

Scandinavian

Frija-Frigg was the wife of Odin, the Father of the Gods. Frija, means "spouse" or "well-beloved." It is clear that many of the gods in this part of the world were given names which were adjectives describing their functions or the gifts they gave to humanity.

Frija-Frigg was the bestower of love, if not sexual intercourse. She gave her name to Friday (in German: Freitag), and the Romans, aware of her attributes, identified her with Venus.

Fish was eaten on a Friday in honor of Frigg, but what is more likely to be the truth of the matter is that fish was *only* eaten on the day of the love goddess, because it was sacred to her.

Frig, Freya, Holda and Hilde were all names of the goddess, and her chief festival was May Day. May Eve, however, was the time of preparation for the celebrations and the arrival of the goddess on the following day. The festival of Beltane, or May Day, was one of sexual love and lasciviousness. An old folk song gives the verse: "If all those young men were like fish in the water, then all those pretty maidens would soon follow after."

The Rite of Pisces

When the Lord of Light has entered the sign of Pisces, prepare your altar and light a pale green candle. This rite begins with a period of contemplation upon the following theme: planet Earth is believed to be 4,600 million years old. But to understand this inconceivable span of time, we must suppose Mother Earth to be a person 46 years of age.

There is no evidence as to how she came into existence, and, although slight clues exist concerning the formative years, it is only at the age of 42 that any kind of development occurred.

One year ago, when the Earth Mother was 45, dinosaurs and other great reptiles appeared on the scene, while mammals came into existence eight months ago. Ape-like people walked the earth during the last two weeks, and at the weekend the most recent ice age covered the globe.

During the last four hours of her life, modern humans walked upon her surface, and in the last hour made a breakthrough with agriculture! A minute ago the industrial revolution was at its height and brought forth the rape of the Earth Mother.

Since we appeared on the earth, we have multiplied our species to plague proportions and have made extinct more than five hundred species of the animal kingdom. Among other untold horrors perpetrated on our fellows, we have plundered, burned and poisoned the vegetable kingdom in our lust for power and our greed for money.

According to the Bible, it is said that the meek shall inherit the Earth. But will the Earth be worth inheriting? One can envisage a new virus, called the "Meek," becoming the scourge of power-mad tycoons who bulldoze their way over the planet!

It is to be hoped that the concerned members of society will win the battle for Mother Earth. And because so many are now aware of the imminent danger, there is every chance of their being successful. Think on all this.

Gaze at the aura of your candle, then close your eyes on the world of form and begin your visualization.

X X X X

When you awaken on the inner planes, you are being gently rocked. It is a most soothing feeling, and you realize, without the shadow of a doubt, that you are, and always have been, protected, cared for and loved!

Your eyes open upon a very strange world indeed! You are resting in a most unusual cradle. It is a great sea-shell, carved in the likeness of two fishes, facing in opposite directions. Your breath emanates from your mouth in the form of opalescent bubbles and you find that you are at the bottom of the sea! You are perfectly at ease in this environment, and being at-one with the vast ocean is extremely comforting and peaceful.

Looking up, you see a dainty foot, showing beneath the hem of a gray-green diaphanous gown, which taps the cradle, rhythmically. The foot is encased in a shoe, embroidered with silver fish scales and iridescent pearls.

The owner of the foot bends over the cradle, the currents in the sea spreading her long hair in a dark halo around her head. The slender neck is graced with a necklace of huge pearls, set in coral, which is carved into the shapes of wondrous sea-creatures. Her wide, gray eyes gaze tenderly upon you, as the eyes of a mother upon her child.

"So, you have come at last!" Her voice has the quality of a running brook and you can hear it quite clearly. She smiles, and you are lost in admiration. It is as though every soul you have loved is present in this being, and you realize that this is the Goddess in yet another guise.

"Yes. You are correct! I am the Mother of All, though few acknowledge me. You are come to the fount of all things to be renewed and regenerated in the waters of life, to undergo a rebirth, with new knowledge, to prepare you for the next round of zodiacal rites. But remember that all returns are as a spiral and continue on a higher, more spiritual level."

The Goddess stops speaking, to play with a shoal of fish which swim in and out of her undulating hair. Her laughter falls like bursting bubbles on your ears, and you join in, stroking the darting fish and shaking hands eight times with a friendly octopus!

"My friend will take you upon this journey." She points a long finger towards a dark shape, emerging from a clump of waving seaweed. The dolphin swims round the Goddess, nudging and pushing her with its snout. She strokes the smooth, shining skin and the dolphin nuzzles greedily at her hand.

"You will be safe with Pepo and he will bring you back when the adventure is over."

Pepo swims up to you and invites you to sit upon his back. You notice that your body weight is much lighter in this element, and standing up, you over-balance and tumble head over heels, much to the delight of your companions!

You are soon moving at speed through the water. It is an exhilarating ride and you feel telepathically close to your friend of the deep.

Pepo swims carefully, so as not to fling you off. He chatters away with peculiar whistles and hoots, to reas-sure you that all is well. You pass through dark tunnels of rock, disturbing fishes of fantastic shapes and colors. Then you dart up, almost to the surface, when the sun-light filters through in a golden haze.

Now, a huge ray flaps past, a great, black shadow, obscuring the opaque, half-light. Pepo shows you the wrecks of galleons on the sea-bed and half-submerged chests of doubloons, worth a king's ransom.

A great hoard of treasure spills from a rotting coffer and Pepo allows you to examine the jewels. Gold bang-les, inlaid with amber, lie with emerald-studded ear-rings and silver bracelets. Rings set with sapphires, dia-monds and pearls wink up at you but are outshone by the blood-red glow of a ruby necklace that may once have graced the white skin of a princess. All these are displayed before your incredulous gaze. Then, a large cray-fish ambles across the sea-bed and the treasure dis-appears in a cloud of powdery sand.

There are cities at the bottom of the sea. Great cas-tles and towers of bygone civilizations have become the homes of fishes and all kinds of denizens of the deep. You walk through streets where long dead people once strode around, intent upon their daily tasks. Pepo plays hide-and-seek among the broken walls of houses, and, snuffling in a corner of what was once a livingroom, he uncovers a child's toy—a doll with one leg missing. He pushes it towards you as a gift, and you thank him with a big hug.

The city is left behind and eventually the dolphin brings you to a dark entrance in a clump of rocks. Pepo waits for you to dismount and you know he will wait for you. He nudges you forward and you float into the cave, surprising a porpoise who lives there.

The cave slopes very gradually upwards and soon you walk out of the water and onto a path made from pebbles embedded in the sand. The passage is filled with phosphorescent light and the air smells strongly of brine. A light breeze caresses your body—which feels unexpectedly heavy after its sojourn in the ocean. All you can hear is your own breathing and the distant shush, shush of water in the cave behind.

A little way along, the passage divides into two— each avenue ending in small, round chambers, barred by curiously wrought gates. The gate on the left is made entirely of horn, while the one on the right is composed of ivory. Above each gate, a relevant inscription, executed in tiny shells, reads, "The Gate of Horn," and "The Gate of Ivory."

The gates are ornamented with scrolls and symbols, and you examine them closely. One is inscribed with many well-known symbols, including those of the various religions and faiths of the world. Those on the other gate, however, are frightening, grotesque shapes and figures, portrayed with staring eyes and cavernous mouths.

The handles of the gates are carved in the likeness of sea horses, and you decide to enter the chamber of the Ivory Gate.

You walk in and close the gate behind you. The room is quite small— much like a womb. Hanging at an angle between the roof and the wall is a large, black mirror. Oval in shape, its frame is of ivory. A couch of alabaster stands in the center of the chamber. It is wrought in the form of two fishes—the sign of Pisces. Sponges packed inside a net provide some comfort, and you sink, thankfully, upon it.

Your vision is drawn directly into the mirror's dark, shadowy surface, and afterwards, it is difficult to know whether you slept, or gazed into the speculum. The visions you experience, however, will never be forgotten.

As each picture rises into your consciousness, you are drawn into its center. You are made to see people stripped of all pretense, without the veneer they adopt in public. All the hidden vices of the world are paraded before you; people dying from the addiction of drugs, children degraded and made to live in cess pools of depravity. Cruelty is shown in all its forms, depicting our greed for money and power.

The plight of animals is revealed—exploited, tortured and killed for material gain or idle curiosity. Whales, seals, elephants, tigers, and all the many species that are at our mercy and unable to fight for their rights of freedom, appear in the mirror. The scenes are all the more harrowing because you are made a part of the life passing through the speculum.

All this and many more unspeakable, monstrous crimes are shown with awful clarity. For this is the Gate of Ivory—the gate of false dreams and desires. You are being confronted by the evil in the world, drawn from the Akashic Record. Yet, even now, despite all the iniquities and crimes, there is always hope. Those who dwell in the darkness of the pit can begin the ascent *whenever they so choose!*

When, at last, the pictures fade, a faint star appears in the mirror – the Star of Hope. Trembling and unable to move for a while, you are vividly aware of the vestiges of another, darker-hued personality that you wore during your incarnations upon this Earth. There are few souls who have not experienced the negative side of zodiacal attributes, for perfection is a state to work towards, through the spiral of evolution.

The more individuals become aware of the spark within and discern, however dimly, the principles of light and truth, the more quickly will the transition occur.

Here, in the dual sign of Pisces, there is a certain freedom to go in either direction, although the Cord of Stars that symbolize the twelve signs of the zodiac show that this freedom is limited in Pisces. Either of the two fishes can swim in any one direction, but it will come to the end of that journey and be pulled up by the Cord. It will then either drag its fellow along with it, or, if the other fish is the stronger of the two, be drawn back to its original position.

This allegory is also true for human beings – as indeed it was meant to be! Until we become fully cognizant of the moral and obligatory laws of the universe, the game of the fishes will go on indefinitely. Evil people will continue to sway the gullible. It is up to enlightened souls to swim strongly in the direction of universal love – the path of peace!

When you are recovered from the ordeal, you depart, closing the gate behind you.[8] Outside, refreshments have been placed ready. Some fluffy, milk-white

---

[8]If you feel that you cannot face the contents of the room of the Gate of Ivory, do not enter it. You will know, instinctively, when you are ready for such a confrontation.

cakes rest upon a large flat shell, and a beaker, made from horn, contains sparkling water. Partaking of them, you wonder what the next room has in store.

Refreshed, you pass through the Gate of Horn. The room is very similar to the first one, except for the couch and the frame of the mirror, which are of ebony.

Reclining on the couch, you notice that the mirror is full of tiny sparks of light. Then you realize that you are seeing into the depths of space! Again, you are drawn into the speculum, but this time it is to become a part of creation on a cosmic scale!

Being in celestial company in the remoteness of infinity creates a feeling of ecstacy, unlike anything you have experienced in the physical body. In fact, you *are* this rapture—it is a part of you—now!

Looking down, you find that your astral body has disappeared! You are now existing as *pure thought* on the manasic or mind level of being! You find that to be without a physical, or an astral form, is not in the least uncomfortable or difficult.

The feeling of bliss continues, and with it comes a yearning to be in this condition forever! There is even dismay at the thought of returning to the Earth! You are content, merely, to be, and to watch the galactic display.

The great Dance of Life is being enacted with the stuff that created our world! How can our speck of a planet be the only one of its kind in the universe? It is important to us because it is our Mother and gave us life, but surely, all this grandeur, this vast stellar miracle, was wrought for more important purposes than to provide Earthlings with a pretty star-spangled sky?

The machinery of the universe whirls and erupts around you. Comets with long fiery tails streak past. Stars are born in a blaze of blue-white flame, and a vast red sun, many times larger than our own, is settling, after billions of years, to a maturity of even greater length. Once a star and flaunting a fiery corona of blasting heat, it speeded through the spectrum colors of orange, green and violet in the breath of a million light years to arrive at its present stage, and a few seconds into its story. Time, as we know it, does not exist here.

There is no sense of movement, and yet you are in motion. Whether up or down, forwards or backwards is impossible to define, and perhaps it is none of these. But, traveling, you are!

The horizon is growing brighter and is filled with a myriad of stars, expanding at an enormous rate in every direction. A White Dwarf rolls into view, dragging a stream of star-stuff in its wake—an immense river of shining silver beads.

Now, you are conscious of a slight tugging and begin to fall, towards what? All around you there is a dimming of vision, as though you are being sucked into a funnel of smoked glass, reducing the view of the galactic extravaganza. It becomes ever darker and you appear to be dropping at an incredible speed—faster and faster.

Then, gradually, the descent slows until it is like that of a bubble falling through air. You emerge from the tunnel into a star-bright sky, such as would be seen from Earth, and find you are floating in your astral body at the center of a vast, silver ring. Dimly, beyond the ring's circumference, you perceive constellations of stars that you recognize as belonging to the sidereal zodiac. Many of these stars are millions of light years distant from the Earth.

Now, rays of light are being put forth by these very constellations from the deeps of space. When the rays reach the silver ring they are held and transmuted into pulsating colors, each one a vibrant shade of the spectrum. The beauty of the sight is awe-inspiring.

Then, something else happens. Slowly, in the medium of stardust, the twelve signs of the zodiac build around the circle until they are superimposed on the spectrum colors. The vision hangs in the heavens like a jewelled mandala, with you—a child of Earth—at its center.

You begin to feel the wholeness of the pattern and comprehend the underlying sense and wisdom of the signs. Each one has a special message to offer, and the twelve, complete, reveal the shining Crown of Glory which is our heritage; a heritage, moreover, whereby we can pursue our journey to the stars!

Now, projecting from the circle of the zodiac come all the gods and goddesses you have met in your astral wanderings. Maat, Venus, Mars, Pan, Mercury, the Discouri, the Virgin, Isis and Osiris, Chiron, Nicholas—the Lord of Death and Regeneration, and the Goddess in her three-fold aspects, all are there to greet you. All, except one. The one you have not yet encountered!

A great laugh shakes the entire structure making the pictures tremble and emit a tinkling sound. And from the place of Pisces, the huge figure of Neptune, the sea-god, manifests. A crown of silver surmounts the long, shaggy hair, and a gleaming trident is grasped in a mighty fist. From his massive shoulders falls a glittering green cloak, embroidered with ribbons of seaweed, and his beard, streaked with sea-foam, is stroked by huge fingers. Eyes, the color of green marbles, appraise the assembly with a tolerant yet insolent stare. It is evident that Neptune considers himself to be as important, if not superior, to the other gods and goddesses. Certainly, he must be regarded as one of the chief founders of life on Earth.

With one easy stride he is at your side and whispering, "Time to go!" He flings the cloak around you, and from the midst of this celestial company, you are carried back, by a god, to the couch in the room beneath the waves.

Neptune explains that the Gate of Horn is the Gate of Dreaming True, and that this is what has happened to you. He escorts you back down the passage and into the water where the faithful Pepo swims to you.

Neptune, also tells you that wherever you go and whatever happens, you may call upon his aid at any time. Then, he is gone, and Pepo is swimming back with you to the cradle-shell.

The Goddess lifts you off the dolphin and holds you, as her child, in a motherly embrace.

"My Darling, you must rest now, after all the adventures you have had. Remember, I am with you always—even to the stars!" She places you lovingly in the cradle and begins to croon a lullaby while tapping the shell with a graceful foot. In spite of yourself, your astral eyes close on the beautiful face with its frame of drifting hair, and you awaken in your chair in front of the altar.

The room is full of the scent of the sea and the sound of running water, as of a brook, issues from your inner ear. It is the Communion of Love, sometimes known as the Brook of Love, purling from the astral plane. In what manner will you return it?

The beginning . . .

Patricia Crowther, a native of Yorkshire, England, has been a witch since 1960, when she was initiated into the craft by Gerald B. Gardner. She is currently a High Priestess of the Great Goddess, as well as being heir to a tradition from Scotland. As a doyenne of the Old Religion, she is one of its leading spokespeople and has lectured widely, initiated covens, and represented Wicca at an international conference in Barcelona, Spain. She has written many books on the subject of Wicca, including *Lid Off the Cauldron* (also published by Samuel Weiser). She recently published her first novel, *Witches Were For Hanging* (Excalibur Press, 1991), and is in the process of writing another.